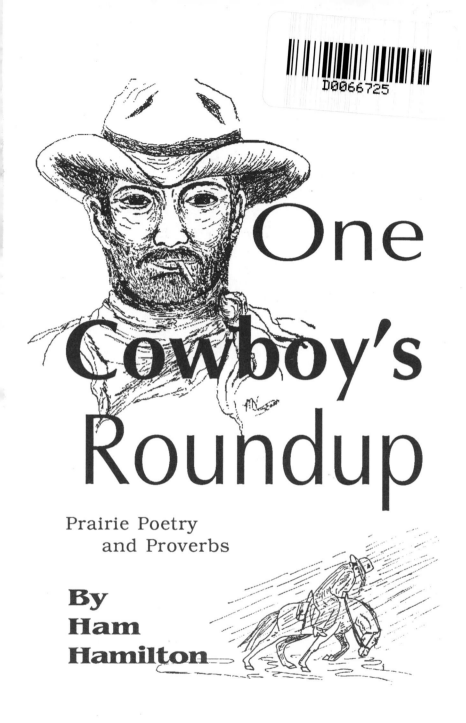

One Cowboy's Roundup

Prairie Poetry
and Proverbs

By
Ham
Hamilton

One Cowboy's Roundup

Illustrations for cover and text by Margaret Stoor

Hamilton, Ham
    One cowboy's roundup / Ham Hamilton.
    p. cm.Preassigned LCCN: 94-61537
    ISBN 0-9643426-1-8

    1. Cowboys--Poetry. 2. Folk poetry--American.   I. Title
PS3558.A4435054   811'.54
                                         QBI94-2378

Published by:
    A Wide Line
    722 Victor Avenue
    Chubbuck, ID 83202-2623

Produced by Frontier Publishing, Seaside, Oregon

Printed in the United States of America

Dedication

===== To Ellie =====

It would take another volume
to express my thanks.

Foreword

I say these poems say what I mean them to say. The publisher says some kind of explanation is required at the beginning of every book. Publishers win.

Over thirty years ago, as a young ranch hand, I sat in a bunkhouse with some old cowboys and heard them recite poetry. How wonderful, I thought, to put one's thoughts and feelings into memorable words. So for nearly thirty years I composed verse and threw it away as unworthy. Some of it was probably better than what is in this volume. All cowboys are intelligent, but this one sometimes isn't too smart.

Cowboys have always participated in gatherings. They gather cattle, they gather personal belongings, and they gather together for social activity. One of these social affairs is a poetry gathering, a group of cowboys composing, reciting, reminiscing.

These poems are my gathering of personal reflections about life on a horse, in a bunkhouse, at a cook shack, among very good men and a few scoundrels, around a fire, too deep in a corral . . . . Deep feelings, sometimes twisted thinking, yearnings, a love of the outdoors of the world's best country, a recognition of God, a hope for better things — at least a smile; all of these should appear somewhere. It must be remembered that cowboys don't lie. But they are natural philosophers and constantly search for larger limits to the truth.

Don't take any of this stuff too seriously. There are three sections, so browse a little. *Tripe* is a little more easily defined as western than *gibberish*. There may be a smile in a prayer here, but there is certainly no attempt to be light-hearted about praying.

Grammar I don't care about; punctuation and spelling just get in the way. Like many other decent ranch hands, profanity and vulgarity are outside my vocabulary. The stuff printed here is made for the Parson to read to his granddaughter. If it is offensive to you, just pay for it and burn it. We will both feel better.

Oh, by the way. . . I tried to cover up the identity of the scoundrels I have met because I don't want to meet them again. If you think you know someone on one of these pages, you are most likely mistaken. But buy him a copy, anyhow.

Ham Hamilton

Contents

Part One

Tripe

and

Tales

The Cowboy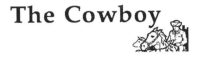

THE COWBOY WAS NEVER A REAL PERSON!
HE WAS MADE UP ON HISTORY'S PAGE.
THERE NEVER WAS A TEN-DOLLAR COW!
AND THERE NEVER WAS A CARE-FREE AGE.

THEY ARE ALL IMAGE DREAMED LONG AGO.
SOMEONE JUST DID FANCY COMPOSING.
WE ALL KNOW BETTER, BUT LOVE IT,
AND CHOOSE TO KEEP ON SUPPOSING.

BUT, IN MY BACK YARD THERE'S A COYOTE;
AT NIGHT SPOTTED HERDS DRIFT MY SKY.
THE COWBOY IS SOLID IN MY MEMORY,
AND HIS SPIRIT RIDES PRETTY NIGH.

SO I WEAR A BIG HAT AND PLAID SHIRT,
AND WEAR BOOTS THAT GIVE ME A GAIT.
I RHYME LIES THAT NEVER DO HARM,
AND PRAY FOR A COWBOY'S FATE!

---

*The dollar in your pocket changes
value every day they hold auction.*

Howdy!

PLEASE LET ME INTRODUCE MYSELF, SO YOU'LL
    KNOW HOW GOOD I AM
'CAUSE MY LIFE'S THE BEST THAT CAN BE WRESTLED
    FROM THE LAND.
MY HOUSE IS MORE THAN SUFFICIENT, IN FEET SIX
    THOUSAND SQUARE,
BUT THE SUMMER HOME IS LARGER SO WE ENTERTAIN
    UP THERE.
MY WIFE IS A LOVELY LADY WHO STILL CAN WEAR HER
    WEDDING DRESS,
HER COUNTENANCE IS PEACEFUL, AND SHE LOVES ME,
    I CONFESS.
MY BOYS HAVE BEEN SUCCESSFUL BOTH IN SCHOOL
    AND IN THEIR TOIL,
WHILE IT IS TRUE THAT NEITHER NOW MAKES A LIVING
    FROM THE SOIL.
ONE'S BOY IS A WASHINGTON LAWYER WHO DOES HIS
    WORK FOR FREE.
THE OTHER IS A PSYCHIATRIST WHO CURES SICK
    PEOPLE, WITHOUT FEE.
MY RANCH CONSISTS OF 97 SECTIONS OF DEEDED,
    FERTILE GROUND,
IT'S PROBABLY THE NICEST PLACE FOR SEVERAL
    STATES AROUND.
I HAVE WATER FLOWING FREELY THROUGH FIVE
    CREEKS ACROSS THE PLACE
EACH ONE HAS LARGE PONDS, AND THERE'S A TROUT
    AND BEAVER LAKE.
THE HAY LAST YEAR WAS SO HEAVY I COULDN'T PUT IT
    UP,
IN FALL I GRAZED THE LAST THREE FIELDS TO GET IT
    EVENED UP.

MY STEERS HAVE ALWAYS TOPPED THE MARKET WHEN
    I DECIDE TO SELL;
THAT'S BECAUSE OF PROVEN BULLS I HAVE, WHICH
    FUNCTION VERY WELL.
I CAN'T COMPLAIN ABOUT MY HUNTING, SKILLS ARE
    ALWAYS UP TO PAR,
I'VE BAGGED A TROPHY BUCK EACH YEAR, FOR FORTY
    YEARS SO FAR.
I TRAVEL WHEN AND WHERE I PLEASE, AND I TRAVEL
    IN EASE AND SLOW.
ANTARCTICA IS NOW THE ONLY PLACE THAT I HAVE YET
    TO GO.

SUCCESS HAS NOT ELUDED ME, I HAVE HEALTH
    THAT'S VERY GOOD,
I EAT STEAKS EVERY DAY, AND BASK IN NEIGHBORLY
    BROTHERHOOD.
I ENJOY MY WEALTH AND LEISURE; I THINK EVERYONE
    SHOULD TRY,
BUT I ALSO UNDERSTAND THAT I'M BLESSED BEYOND
    THE AVERAGE GUY.
LIFE IS SUCH A WONDERFUL TIME, ONE BIG PLEASANT
    SURPRISE,
WHEN ONE IS A COWBOY POET, WHO GETS PAID FOR
    TELLING LIES!

---

*It is hard to hear anything when
your ears are plugged with pride*

Doggie Diner

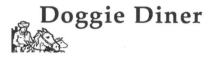

THE BIG DOG WAS WHITE-EYED AND SPOTTED
AND HE SHOWED A WIDE STREAK OF MEAN.
HE WOULDN'T BACK OFF FROM ANYTHING.
HE WAS A TOUGH COW MAN'S DREAM.
HE WOULD OFTEN SIT ON HIS HAUNCHES,
SHIFTING WEIGHT BETWEEN HIS FRONT FEET.
ANYTHING MOVING WAS SEEN AS A MEAL,
AND THAT DOG HAD APPETITE FOR RED MEAT.
HE WAS OWNED BY A GROUCHY OLD RANCHER,
WHO GRUBBED A LIVING BEST AS HE COULD,
A MAN MARRIED TO A BIG HEARTED WOMAN,
WHO "MADE DO," AS A GOOD WOMAN SHOULD.
THEY DIDN'T HAVE MUCH THAT WAS FANCY,
NO RUG EVER COVERED THEIR FLOOR.
DISHES WERE PLAIN, TABLE WAS SPARSE;
POVERTY SEEMED PARKED AT THEIR DOOR.
BUT THEY NEVER WHINED ABOUT BEING POOR,
THEY SHARED WHAT LITTLE THEY HAD.
KEEPING FEED FOR THAT DOG WAS A CHORE.
HE OFTEN ATE MEAT THAT WENT BAD.
IT WASN'T THAT THEY HAD SO MUCH MEAT,
BUT THAT THE DOG KILLED NOW AND THEN.
IT WAS EASIER TO HANG UP THE KILL,
THAN TO TRY TO KEEP THE DOG IN A PEN.

So ALONG COMES A STRANGER ONE EVENING
AS CHORES WERE DONE FOR THE DAY,
AND HE WANTS SOME REST FOR HIS MOUNT,
AND SOMEWHERE HIS BODY CAN LAY.
THE WOMAN OFFERS TO SHARE SUPPER, TOO.
SHE WARNED THAT IT WOULDN'T BE MUCH.
HE WAS WARMED BY THE OFFER OF FOOD,

AND BY HER HOSPITALITY, TOUCHED.
THE DOG KNEW THAT HIS FEED WOULD SHRINK
AND HUNGER WOULD TUG AT HIS GUTS.
HE GAVE A WHITE STARE AT THE STRANGER
THAT PORTENDED OF ILL FROM THE MUTT.
THE RANCHER GAVE THE MAN THE WASH BOWL
AND REQUESTED THAT HE TIDY UP A BIT.
THESE FOLKS WERE PLAIN, BUT THEY WERE CLEAN,
BODY ODORS GAVE THAT CUR CROSSBRED A FIT.
SUPPER WAS SET TO THE BIG PINE BOARD,
A LARGE BOWL AND A SPOON FOR EACH ONE.
TWO UTENSILS APIECE WAS ALL THAT SET OUT,
FOR OF ANYTHING ELSE, THEY HAD NONE.
THE DOG WAS ALERT TO THE PROCEEDINGS
AND HE TOOK A PLACE AT ONE SIDE.
HIS CHIN WAS EVEN WITH THE TABLE BOARD,
AND HAIR SHED FROM FROM HIS SPOTTED HIDE.

THE STRANGER TRIED TO BE PATIENT, CALM,
KEEP FRAYED NERVES UNDER CONTROL,
BUT SEEING THAT DOG SHIFT ON HIS FEET
KEPT HIS MIND FROM APPOINTED BOWL.
THE DOG ROTATED HIS STARES, AND SHIFTS;
THE DISCOMFORTED MAN GAVE A JERK;
GRUMPY OLD RANCHER SWORE AT THE DOG,
WHICH DUCKED IT'S HEAD AS IT SHIRKED.
ALL WAS QUIET AT THE TABLE FOR A MOMENT,
BUT SAYING RELAXED WOULD BE LIES.
MAN AND BEAST WERE COMPETING FOR FOOD
IN COUNTRY WHERE THE HUNGRY ONE DIES.
TALK PICKED UP AS THEY EMPTIED THEIR BOWLS
AND THE MEN AND WOMAN CONVERSED,
ABOUT WHAT WAS THE COUNTRY'S GOINGS-ON
AND WHAT WAS GETTIN' BETTER, OR WORSE.
BUT THE BIG DOG SHOWED HIS NERVOUSNESS
AND UNSETTLED THE STRANGER SOME.
THE DOG WAS NOW CROWDING HIS ELBOW

AND THE GROWLING GOT HIM UNDONE.
HE ASKED THAT THE DOG BE PUT OUTSIDE-
THAT HE BE GRANTED SOME SPACE.
THE RANCHER SAID THAT THE DOG WOULD STAY
FOR THIS WAS HIS NORMAL PLACE.
THE WOMAN SEEMED TO WISH THINGS DIFFERENT,
BUT FAILED TO SPEAK HER FULL MIND.
SHE WAS USED TO THE DOG IN THE HOUSE
AND REQUESTED THE MAN TO UNWIND.

THE STRANGER COULDN'T HANDLE THE PRESSURE;
HE BURST IN AN EMOTIONAL DISPLAY.
HE WANTED TO KNOW OF CANINE INTENT,
AND HOW TO KEEP THE BIG DOG AT BAY.
"HE'LL BE ALL RIGHT," SAID THE RANCHER,
"IF YOU WILL JUST DO AS YOU'RE TOLD.
THE PROBLEM IS VERY PLAIN TO THOSE WHO KNOW;
YOU HAVE BEEN EATING OUT OF HIS BOWL."

====================================

*Sacrifice is like a pup — often called
for and often unwelcome.*

====================================

It's Enough

GIVE 'EM A ROPE AND SADDLE,
A STRING OF HORSES HE CAN RIDE,
AND IT'S A DAMNED POOR COWBOY
WHO WON'T BE SATISFIED.

THE WORST THING FOR A COWBOY
IS TO GIVE THAT MAN A HOME;
YA WANTA KEEP HIM FOLLERIN' COWS
WHEREVER THEY MAY ROAM.

OUT ON THE ROLLIN' PRAIRIE
THERE'S GRASSES FOR A BED,
AND AT DAYBREAK EVERY MORNING
THERE'S A BRONCO TO BE FED.

THERE'S MILE AND MILES OF RIDIN'
TO CHECK THE COWS AND MILLS.
A MAN WILL NEVER GET 'ER DONE
AT HOME, A' SITTIN' STILL.

---

*A true working man hasn't time to
stand at the dice table.*

February

THINGS JUST COULDN'T BE NO WORSER.
NOTHING COULD REACH FURTHER DOWN.
WE ALL HAVE SOME GRUMP ON THE INSIDE
AND OUTSIDE WE'RE SHOWIN' SOME FROWN.

HORSES BUCK HARD CAUSE OF CHILLY.
MULES KICK BOTH RANCHER AND TRACE.
BREAKFAST WASN'T READY THIS MORNIN'.
THERE'S FROST ALL OVER THE PLACE.

WAGON HUB GREASE HAS GOT STIFFENED.
SLEIGH RUNNERS SHOWS UP WITH RUST.
THE COWS HAVE DRIFTED TO NEIGBORS,
WHICH IS WHY THE FENCE IS A BUST.

THE HAY'S BEEN EATEN BY MULE DEER.
THE GRAINERY'S LEAKING TO MICE.
MY SADDLE IS SHOWING SOME MILDEW.
I SLEPT POOR IN A BED FULL OF LICE.

THE MORTGAGE IS DUE WITH THE BANKER.
BABY'S NEEDING FRESH MILK AND CLOTHES.
I AIN'T SEEN A DOLLAR FOR S' LONG
THAT SERENITY IS ONLY A POSE.

THE PREACHER WANTS BIGGER DONATIONS.
THE MERCHANT SAYS TO PAY ON THE BILL.
MY SEED GRAIN GOT DAMP LAST WEEK BUT
THE SPRING IS FROZE UP, ON THE HILL.

MY WOMAN'S IN BED WITH THE SNIFFLES.
SHE DRANK THE CORN BREW AS A CURE,
SO I GOT NONE LEFT FOR MY WORRIES,
AND THE OLD BARN IS FULL OF MANURE.

THE SOW LAID ON THE ONE PIG SHE FARROWED.
THE SHE-DOG IS FEEDING NINE PUPS.
A COYOTE HOWLS IN THINKING OF CALVIN'.
THE WELL'S FROZE; NO WATER COMES UP.

I KNOW THAT IT COULDN'T GET WORSER
BUT IT AIN'T THE END, JIST A FLOP.
UNTIL THE GROCER QUITS TAKING MONEY,
THIS OLD WORLD AIN'T COME TO A STOP.

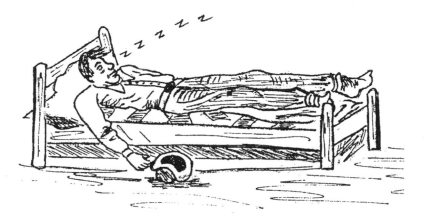

Cow Watchin'

WE STAND ALONG THE CORRAL RAILS IN SUN OF A
BRIGHT SPRING DAY.
LIESURE DROOPS FROM MOUTHS AS SPRIGS OF NEW
BROME HAY.
WE LIKE TO SLOWLY CONTEMPLATE WHAT NEXT WE
HAVE TO DO.
WE'VE PLENTY TIME, THERE'S LOTS OF US, THEY ARE
ONLY FEW.
IT RELAXES US JUST TO WATCH THEM, WITHOUT A
CARE TO TOTE,
RELAXED IN SPRNGTIME WARMTH, SCRATCHIN' ITCHES
IN THEIR COAT.
SEEMS AN EVER-MOVIN' MOUTH IS THEIR MOST
TREASURED TOOL,
'CAUSE THEY SELDOM SWALLOW, AND BROWN JUICES
OFTEN DROOL.
THEY COMMUNICATE IN MUTED TONES FIT TO
NATURE'S QUIET WAY,
'CEPT PASSING WARNIN' WHEN THEIR YOUNG COME
TOWARD HARM'S WAY.
GRUNTS AN' SHAKIN' HEADS GIVE EMPHASIS, WHERE IT
NEEDS BE PUT,
WHO CAN EVER INTERPRET THEIR LOW MOANS, OR A
STOMPING FOOT?
WE BOTH LIKE KNOWING THAT THE HORSES ARE
HOBBLED OFF A PACE.
ONE OF US, THEN, ISN'T FORCED TO RIDE, THE OTHER
ISN'T CHASED.
IF ALL ANIMALS USED THE SAME LANGUAGE TO MAKE
MEANINGS BARE,
WHAT WOULD BE SAID 'TWEEN US, THE COWS, AND
THOSE MEN OVER THERE?

Cussick Creek

I SAW THE CANYON OF CUSSICK CREEK
AS I CAME OFF THE BENCH DOWN EAST.
NOTHING STIRRED IN THE SAGE AT ALL
AS I OBSERVED FROM SADDLED BEAST.

BUT A SCENE PLAYED OUT IN FERTILE MIND
OF MEN AND MULES AND COWS,
AND WORDS FORMED ON A MENTAL PAGE
OF WHAT WAS DONE, AND HOW.

AND I SENSED THAT I HAD A POEM
THAT WOULD LEAVE EMOTIONS STIRRED.
THE PROBLEM IS, I FORGOT THE THING
AND CAN'T RECALL ONE WORD!

High Steaks

An OLD BULL HANGS UPSIDE DOWN IN A DIRTY
    SLAUGHTER HOUSE.
HIS HEAD BLEEDS IN A GUTTER; DEAD EYES STARING
    AT A MOUSE.
THEY JERKED HIS HIDE AROUND, CUT HIS GUTS FOR
    SURGEON'S STRINGS.
HIS TONGUE IS HANGING ON A HOOK WITH ASSORTED
    OTHER THINGS.
HE HAD BEEN A GALANT LOVER IN THE PASTURE IN HIS
    YOUTH,
HE'D BEEN FED THE SWEETEST FEEDS THAT DIDN'T
    NEED A TOOTH.
THEY HAD PAMPERED HIM IN MAJESTY AND ALLOWED
    THE FINEST COWS,
ASSURED HIS HAY WAS CLEAN AND BRIGHT, CHOSEN
    DAILY FROM THE MOW.
HE WAS GIVEN WOODEN BREAK, AND BARN, TO
    SHELTER FROM WINTER WIND.
HIS COAT WAS CURRIED BY THE YOUTH FOR THE FAIRS
    THEY ENTERED IN.
BUT A YOUNGER BULL OF BIGGER BONE BECAME HERD
    SIRE JUST LAST YEAR
AND RANCHERS HAVEN'T ANY HEART, AND DON'T HOLD
    ONE BULLOCK DEAR.
SO THEY PUT HIM ON THE AUCTION BLOCK FOR
    WHATEVER HE WOULD BRING,
AND PRICES SHOUTED OUT WERE SUCH THAT MADE
    HIS LOST PRIDE STING.
HE WASN'T FOUND WORTH NEAR AS MUCH AS A
    CANNER-CUTTER COW,
AND HIS HORNS DIDN'T MATTER MUCH TO THE
    SLAUGHTER MAN RIGHT NOW.

THEY PENNED HIM IN A CAR WITH OTHER BULLS WITH
    A BITING DOG,
AND THAT CAR WAS RIGHT DRAFTY, AND BEHIND A
    SMELLY CAR OF HOGS.
AND THE NOISE OF RUMBLING RAIL CARS WOULD ONLY
    PALE IN TIME
TO THE DIN OF CHAINS AND SHOUTING IN THE
    SLAUGHTER'S SLIME.
THE BULL HAD LOTS OF TIME TO THINK, IF THAT IS
    WHAT BULL'S DO
WHEN CHIPS ARE DOWN, AND A GRAND LONG LIFE IS
    NEARLY THROUGH.
HE COULD THINK ABOUT HIS BROTHER WHO HAD
    PRECEDED HIM IN DEATH,
A YOUNG STEER IN HIS PRIME, SLAUGHTERED AT HIS
    VERY BEST.
STEERS NEVER GAIN THE WEIGHT OF THEIR BULLISH
    OLD HALF BROTHERS,
CAUSE LIVES ARE ALTERED WHILE JUST CALVES,
    BESIDE THEIR MOTHERS.
THE SALE OF MEAT IS PRICED THE SAME, NONE CAN
    TELL THE TWO APART.
ONE PAY'S AS DEARLY FOR BULL OR STEER; ROAST, OR
    SHANK, OR HEART.
THIS BULL WAS TAKEN TO HIS DEATH BEFORE
    MEANING HAD COME CLEAR;
IS A STEER A CUT BELOW A BULL, OR A BULL A CUT
    BEYOND A STEER?

The Buyer

WOULD YOU BUY STOCK FROM A SHAKEN MAN?
WOULD YOU HELP SETTLE A SALE?
WE AREN'T ASKING FOR A TOKEN BUY
OR MERCHANDISE SENT THROUGH THE MAIL.

WE HAVE A MAN WITH UNNEEDED STOCK,
PURCHASED IN ERR OF A SORT.
FIFTEEN HUNDRED HEAD OF COWS
AIN'T NOTHING AT WHICH TO SNORT!

HE WANTED TO KNOW HOW AUCTIONS WORKED,
SO HE SAT SILENT AND CALM.
HE WATCHED CLOSE AS THE ACTION WENT
WHERE THE BIDDERS WAVED A PALM.

PRICES JUMPED UP WITH THE BIDDING
VOICES RAISED AND THEN HUSHED.
THREE MEN ASSISTED THE AUCTIONEER
IN KEEPING THE BUSINESS RUSHED.

A FULL HUNDRED PENS OF LIVESTOCK
MADE IT THROUGH THE RING,
AND THE AUCTIONEER THOUGHT THE MAN
WAS BIDDING ON EVERYTHING

AND IT WAS A SHOCK TO OTHER BUYERS
THAT NO COWS WOULD BE THEIRS,
BUT WOULD BE THE ASSETS IN CONTROL
OF THE MAN OF SILENT AIRS.

THE STRANGER FELT GOOD AS THE AUCTIONEER
WINKED AT THE END OF EACH ROUND.
HE THEN LEARNED AT THE END OF THE SALE
THAT HE'D BOUGHT EVERY COW ON THE GROUND.

HE PAID THE PRICE FOR FEEDING THE STOCK
AND WATER FOR A COUPLE OF DAYS.
BUT HE'S LOOKING HARD FOR BUYERS NOW
AND CARES A LOT HOW THEY PAY.

LESSONS HE LEARNS ARE NOT SPOKEN OUT LOUD
FOR HE IS DEAF IN BOTH EARS.
HE HELD HIS HAND AT THE BACK OF HIS HEAD
TO HEED THE VOICE OF A FAST AUCTIONEER!

Cattle Auction

I'M A Cowman

I'M A COWMAN. I WAS THAT WAY WHEN BORN.
THERE'S NO WAY TO BE OTHERWISE.
NOTHING ELSE COULD I BE!

I NEED A SHEEP. EACH MAN MUST HAVE A LAMB.
THERE IS NO WAY TO DO WITHOUT.
THE MUTTON IS THE KEY!

I KEEP A SHEEP. A TREND MY DAD INSPIRED.
THERE IS NO WAY WITHOUT A LAMB,
ITS PRESENCE SAVES YOUR BUTT.

I'M A COWMAN. MY DADDY TAUGHT ME WELL.
THERE'S NO WAY BUT TO GET A SHEEP
AND FEED 'EM TO YOUR MUTT!

---

*Say something for the sake of
argument and you'll have one.*

The New Hand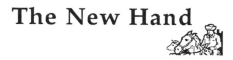

WE GREETED THE MAN, SHOWED HIM A BUNK,
MADE SURE HIS BEDROLL WAS GOOD,
GAVE HIM A TOUR OF CORRALS AND BARN,
MADE WELCOME AS MUCH AS WE COULD.

HE SPOKE SOFT, THOUGH LITTLE HE SPOKE
OF RANGES HE'D RIDDEN OR SEEN.
HE DIDN'T TALK BIG OF HOW HE COULD RIDE
AND NEVER SAID ANYTHING MEAN.

HE WENT SLOW AS HE PICKED OUT HIS STRING;
GAVE GOOD CARE TO TACK AND TO HORSE.
HE DID EVERYTHING WITH EXTRA THOUGHT
AND HE AVOIDED ALL USES OF FORCE.

IT LOOKED LIKE THERE WAS NO BETTER MAN
TO HELP WITH CHORES OR A DRIVE.
HE SHOWED A KNACK FOR USING THE TOOLS
THAT KEPT OWNER AND RANCH HAND ALIVE.

BUT WE SOON KNEW THAT SOMETHING WAS UP
THAT WOULDN'T MAKE A GOOD FIT.
STRAIN IN THE AIR AS THICK AS DOG HAIR
PREVENTED HIS MAKING A HIT.

THERE WAS NO SADNESS LOST ON THE MAN.
WE GLADLY WAVED HIM GOODBYE
WITHOUT A THOUGHT OF WHERE HE WENT,
OR WHERE HIS FUTURE WOULD LIE.

HIS LINGO DIDN'T HOLD UP VERY LONG,
NOT LONG DID WE GIVE HIM A HOPE.
THAT MAN SPOKE OF HIS BOOTS AS HIS SHOES,
AND HAD WOOL CAUGHT UP IN HIS ROPE.

Good Health

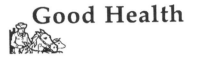

I AM FREE OF ALL BRUISES AND BANGS.
WHENEVER ASKED, I SAY "HEARTY AND HALE,
I'M FEELING GOOD, RIGHT HEALTHY THANKS,
I HAVEN'T EVEN THE SLIGHTEST HANGNAIL."

I'VE BEEN AWAY FROM THE CATTLE CHUTES,
SO I'VE NO SHOULDER SPRAINS OR SPLINTERS.
THE SEASON HAS CHANGED TO WARM A WHILE;
IT'S GOOD-BYE TO WINTER CHILLS AND SHIVERS.

FENCES ON THE PLACES AROUND ARE REPAIRED,
THEREFORE, NO WIRE CUTS OR CALLOUS SPLITS.
THE BRINDLE MILK COW WAS RECENTLY SOLD;
THERE'S NO MUSCLE STRAIN FROM PULLING TEATS.

COWS THESE DAYS ARE TREATED IN A METAL CHUTE,
NEAR THE DRAINED CORRAL WHERE THEY ARE BORN.
SO I DON'T HAVE THE OLD-TIME TRIBULATIONS
WHILE DOCTORING ROPE BURNS AND RIDING SORES.

I BEEN TRULY BEHAVIN' 'CAUSE MONEY'S SHORT,
BUT NOTE THAT MY HEALTH IS UP FROM "LOUSY".
AND HERE I AM IN TOWN TEN WHOLE DAYS
WITHOUT DRUNKENNESS AND THE DROWSIES.

YOU KNOW THAT IT IS NOT A NORMAL THING
WHEN I'M FREE OF THE JUMPYS AND JERKS.
BUT I BEEN THIS WAY FOR TWO FULL WEEKS.
STILL, I WISH I WASN'T OUT OF WORK.

The Evening Visit

A LANKY COWMAN STOOD IN THE DOORWAY
AND LEANED UP AGINST THE JAMB.
YOU COULD TELL BY THE DROOP OF HIS CIGARETTE
THAT HE DIDN'T GIVE A DAMN.
HE SMILED REAL SLOW ON THE RIGHT SIDE,
WITH DISDAIN ON THE REST OF HIS FACE.
HE NOTICED THE GALS IN THE VERY LARGE HALL,
WEARING SATIN, AND VELVET, AND LACE.
THE PLACE CAME TO A VIRTUAL STANDSTILL,
JIST RIGHT FOR A PAINTER'S STILL LIFE.
COMPLEXIONS WENT PALE; NERVES TOTALLY FAILED.
THE DEALER PUT A CASE ON HIS DICE!
THERE WASN'T ANYONE WANTED TO ARGUE.
THE PLACE WENT QUIET AS CHURCH.
THE ONLY SOUND WAS THE BAR MAN'S SIGH,
LIKE AN AUTUMN WIND THROUGH A BIRCH.
THEN THE COWMAN WENT SOLEMN AS JUDGEMENT,
STOOD STRAIGHT AND TAUT AS DRAWN BOW,
SLIPPED OUT IN THE DARKNESS AND VANISHED.
WHAT HE WANTED, WE NEVER WILL KNOW!

Homestead Hiring

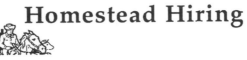

MY FAMILY SAID THAT RANCHING WAS TOUGH
    BUSINESS,
THOUGH WE OWNED SIX SECTIONS OF IRRIGATED
    GRASS.
SO WHEN THE OLD MAN DIED AND I INHERITED THE
    PLACE,
I WAS FIXING TO SHOW 'EM AND NOT TO FEEL
    DISGRACE.

I TOOK SOME CASH; WENT AND BOUGHT A BIGGER
    RANCH
WITH CORRALS AND LOADING PENS ON THE H & W
    BRANCH,
AND GOOD HAY AND RANGE, AND SHELTERED CALVING
    GROUND,
AND BUNK HOUSE, BARN AND COOK SHACK CLOSE
    AROUND.

AND THEN I WENT TO TOWN AND HIRED EIGHT
    STRONG BOYS
WHO KNEW COWS AND MACHINES WERE WORK
    INSTEAD OF TOYS.
I WATCHED BEFORE I HIRED; THERE WASN'T A CARD
    PLAYED
AMONG THEM, AND SOME COULD WRITE; ONE EVEN
    PRAYED.

NO MAN WAS HIRED THAT WORE HIS SPURS ON THE
    STREET;
IN FACT, EACH HAD TO HAVE WORN BOOTS UPON HIS
    FEET.
I GOT NO DRUNKS OR BAR GIRL PROBLEMS ONE
    COULD SEE.
OTHER MEN MADE BIG MISTAKES IN HIRING, BUT NOT
    ME.

I GOT THEM HOME AND SETTLED, AND THEY LOOKED
   CLEAN.
THEY WERE COURTEOUS AT THE TABLE; NEVER, EVER
   MEAN.
MY HORSES WERE BEST-TENDED OF THREE ADJOINING
   STATES.
STILL, I SEEMED TO HAVE MET A RANCHER'S GHASTLY
   FATE.

TROUBLE WAS, MY COWS WEREN'T TENDED PROPERLY
   AT ALL.
I COULD SEE BIG TROUBLE BEFORE ROUNDUP IN THE
   FALL.
MY GOOD BOYS WERE TIRED, BUT THE WORK WAS
   NEVER DONE,
AND IT WASN'T CAUSE OF LAZY, OR FROM THEM
   HAVING FUN.

THESE GUYS STAYED AWAKE AT NIGHT, SELDOM
   WENT TO BED,
ALWAYS ASKED FOR PAPER; WATCHED HOW THINGS
   WERE SAID.
I FOUND THE PROBLEM, SMART MEN WOULD HAVE
   KNOWN IT;
I HADN'T HIRED ONE COWHAND, BUT A LOUSY BUNCH
   OF POETS.

*A smart man learns when his
neighbor gets jailed.*

Rodeo Free

I'M AN ENTERTAINER BRINGIN' CLEAN FUN AND JOY,
AN AMERICAN NATURAL, KNOWN AS "RODEO COWBOY".
A STABLE SYMBOL OF THE WILD OLD WEST, YOU SEE,
CAUSE I'M ON MY OWN, AND FREE AS ONE CAN BE.

I TAKE CHOICE WITH MY CHANCES WHEREVER I GO,
NO ONE CAN TELL ME WHAT TO DO, OR HOW SO.
I'M LIKELY TO MOVE AS I WANT TO, SIT AS I CAN,
INDEBTED MOST LIKELY, BEHOLDEN NO MAN.

THERE WILL BE SOMEONE TO STAKE MY JACKPOT
    ATTEMPT
BECAUSE SUPERIOR SKILLS DON'T MAKE ENTRY
    EXEMPT.
ON THE BRONCO I'M RAKING AND FURIOUSLY FANNING.
ON THE GROUND, IT'S OFTEN PAWN SHOP OR
    PANHANDLING.

I EAT PRETTY GOOD 'CAUSE I CAN LOCATE THE
    GARDENS,
AVOIDING TALL FENCES AND LOUD CANINE
    GUARDIANS.
THE SHOW MOVES WITH THE SEASON, 'CROSS THE
    NATION,
SO I CAN CHOOSE 'TWEEN SLIM PICKIN'S AND
    STARVATION.

MOVING TAKES NO PASSPORT; I'M FREE AS A BREEZE.
I JUST PICK UP MY SADDLE, AS MOVE AS I PLEASE.
WHEN I TRAVEL I GO IN THE STYLE THAT I LIKE,
I CAN HIJACK A FRIEND OR CHOOSE TO HITCH HIKE.

I LIKE BEING OUT DOORS AND CLOSE TO LIVESTOCK.
WHEN DARKNESS FALLS, AND THE ARENA GETS
    LOCKED,
I'M MOM'S GOOD BOY AND STAY AWAY FROM THE
    BROTHEL,
CHOOSING INSTEAD A HAYSTACK OR A FLEABAG
    HOTEL.

I'M FREE. I MAY NOT HAVE EVERY THING YOU DO,
BUT I DON'T HAVE PAYMENTS AND MORTGAGES DUE.
MY HAT SHIELDS FROM RAIN; I WEAR PRETTY LEGGIN'S;
WHO CARES THAT I GOT 'EM BORROWIN' OR BEGGIN'?

I DON'T HAVE TO COMPETE; I CAN ALWAYS GO HOME.
BUT I'D LIKE TO DO IT WITH A DIME OF MY OWN.
THE DOCTORS SAY I'VE HAD AN INTERESTING PAST
AND OFFER CHOICE OF SLING, STRAP, CRUTCH OR
    CAST.

I'M GETTING OLDER, SO I MUST SOON DECIDE
IF MY LAST SHOW WILL BE TO ROPE OR TO RIDE.
I'D LIKE A GOOD SHOWING, BUT BE IT BULL OR A
    STEER,
LIKELY, ME OR MY ROPE WILL BE THROWN FREE AND
    CLEAR!

---

*Pleasure comes from other folks,
happiness is in your own heart, and
God hands out joy.*

The Railroad Cow

SHE AMBLED AMONG THE OTHER COWS BEIN'
   GATHERED,
DISAPPEARANCE IS WHAT SHE WOULD HAVE
   RATHERED.
SHE DIDN'T WANT A MAN TO READ HER EAR TAG,
OR BE PRODDED ALONG BY THE MAN RIDING DRAG.

WEARING NEARLY IDENTICAL COLORS, WHITE AND
   RED,
SHE WAS MARKED THE SAME AS ALL FIVE HUNDRED
   HEAD.
BUT HER TRAITS STOOD OUT FOR EXPERIENCED
   HANDS,
THE MEN RIDING ALONG AND READING HER BRAND.

WATCHING COWS MOTHER CALVES SHOWED HER
   CRIME
AND UNCOVERED THE BOVINE SIN OF ALL TIME.
SHE'D GONE BEYOND WHERE A RANCHER CAN LAUGH.
THAT RAILROAD COW HAD COME IN WITHOUT CALF.

SHE HAD EATEN GRASS WITHOUT LOANING A TEAT
TO A FAT YOUNG AMIMAL DESTINED FOR MARKET.
WELL, SOME FOLKS SAY SHE COULD HAVE GONE.
NOT REALLY, 'CAUSE OF HOW HER BRAND WAS PUT ON.

THERE WAS SEVEN BRANDS WELL MIXED IN THE
    HERD,
IRONED ON TIGHT, AND STATE BRAND BOOK
    REFERRED.
BUT HER'S WASN'T AMONGST THEM; SHE HAD DENSE
SCRAMBLES OF MARKS THAT DIDN'T MAKE SENSE.

SOME YEARS BEFORE, A TRAIN STOPPED ON THE
    TRACK
WAITING FOR CLEARANCE OF SOME THINGS OUT OF
    WACK.
AND THE DOOR LOCK OF A STOCK CAR CAME UNDONE,
AND OUT JUMPS YOUNG STOCK - HEREFORDS EVERY
    ONE.

ALL COWS WERE GATHERED, BUT WITH NO CHUTE TO
    RELOAD,
THE LOCAL AUCTION SOLD THEM AS LESS THAN CAR
    LOAD.
THE TRAIN HAD MOVED ON, AND WITH NO ONE TO
    BLAME,
THE RAILROAD PAID THE SHIPPER TO SETTLE THE
    CLAIM.

THE RAILROAD REVIEWED PAPERS REQUIRED BY THE
    LINE.
EVERYTHING WAS NEAT, AND FINAL SETTLEMENT
    SIGNED.
TWO MONTHS LATER THIS YOUNG COW SHOWS ON THE
    LAND,
AND NO ONE IN TWENTY COUNTIES KNOWS OF HER
    BRAND.

THE BRAND INSPECTOR LOOKS HER HIDE OVER FIVE
WAYS,
AND SAYS SHE DON'T HAVE A LEGAL PLACE SHE CAN
GRAZE.
SO, SHE IS EATING GRASS OF THEIR PRODUCTIVE
COWS,
AND THE RANCH WANTS RID OF HER CARCASS RIGHT
NOW.

THE INSPECTOR SAYS DON'T SELL A COW THAT AIN'T
YOURS
AND GOOD BEEF AIN'T SCARCE ON A RANCH; DON'T
BUTCHER.
THE RAILROAD MEN SAY THAT ALL THE CLAIMS BEEN
SETTLED,
AND THEY DON'T OWN COWS, EVEN THEIR HORSES ARE
METAL.

AND THE RANCH SAYS THE COW JUST ISN'T WELCOME
A HALF,
UNTIL THEY CAN SEE THAT SHE'S GROWING A CALF.
NOW A CALF HAS A MARKET IN MOST PARTS OF THIS
LAND,
AND A MAVERICK ON YOUR PLACE IS LEGAL TO BRAND.

SO THEY GIVE HER A PARDON, 'CAUSE IT CAN BE SEEN
THEY'LL HAVE THE YOUNG ONE WHEN IT HAS BEEN
WEANED.
AND THAT YOUNG COW HAD HERSELF A PLACE ON THE
RANGE
AND THINGS SEEMED TO BE CALMING DOWN FOR A
CHANGE.

AND IT WAS PEACE AND QUIET UNTIL EARLY SPRING
WHEN SHE CALVES A BULL, A BIG HUSKY THING,
THEY CASTRATE AND BRAND THE LITTLE MAVERICK,
FOR A FEW MONTH'S FEED, THAT DOES THE TRICK.

AND THEN THE FIGHT STARTS AGAIN. THE BRAND
  INSPECTOR
SEZ DON'T SELL WHAT AIN'T YOURS; YOU BETTER NOT
  BUTCHER.
AND THE RAILROAD SEZ THEIR BUSINESS IS JUST TO
  RUN TRAINS,
AND THEY LOOKED IN THE FILE AND THE'VE SETTLED
  ALL CLAIMS.

AND THE RANCH SEZ THAT THAT COW EATS THEIR
  PRECIOUS GRASS
UNTIL THEY DISCOVER, THAT FALL, THAT SHE CARRIES
  A CALF.
AND SHE GETS A PARDON, AND THEY CLAIM THE CALF
  WHEN BORN,
AND THEY BRAND THE MAVERICK; YET HER BRAND
  THEY SCORN.

THE COW SEEMS TO THINK THAT HER WORLDLY
  SALVATION
DEPENDS UPON THE OLD HERD BULL'S SUMMER
  FLIRTATION.
SHE DOESN'T KNOW SHE'S USELESS FOR GOLD OR FOR
  MEAT,
'TIL SOMEONE'S PERFORMED A MIRACLE BRAND-
  READING FEAT.

AND THE INSPECTOR IS WATCHING FOR FRESH
  ROUGH HIDES
BEING SOLD ANYWHERES, OR RAIL FENCE-HUNG TO
  DRY.
HE DOESN'T EVER WANT TO SEE THAT POOR BRAND
  AGAIN.
BUT HIS MIND SAYS SEEING IT DEAD WOULD BE SIN.

HE DOESN'T LIKE SEEING THE POOR BRAND ON THE
  HOOF;

A RENDERING PLANT FIND WOULD PUT HIM THROUGH
    THE ROOF.
AND THE RAILROAD MEN HAVE FORGOTTEN ABOUT
    ANYONE'S COWS,
BECAUSE ALL CLAIMS ARE SETTLED AS THE BUDGET
    ALLOWS.

YOU SEE, THEY HAVE NO INTEREST IN SEEING YEARS
    BACK,
'CAUSE THEY DON'T OWN COWS, THEY RUN CARS DOWN
    THE TRACK.
AND THE RANCH WANTS THE WHOLE THING TO
    SUDDENLY PASS
WITHOUT A STRANGE COW CONTINUING TO EAT AT
    THEIR GRASS.

SO, I'M ON THE PLACE AS A BRAND NEW HAND WHEN I
    HEAR
BOSS, "THE RAILROAD COW IS TO BE FOUND OVER
    HERE".
AND THERE WAS A TIME OF DULL MUMBLING OF SORTS
UNTIL "SHE AIN'T GOT A CALF" WAS THE FINAL RETORT.

AND THEN THE DUNG OF THREE CORRALS HIT THE
    FAN,
AND THE INSPECTOR GETS CALLED TO READ HER
    AGAIN.
BUT THIS TIME THEY CLIP THE HAIR OFF HER SIDE
AND THEY SEE EVEN MORE BRAND MARKS ON HER
    HIDE.

EVERY RASCAL IN THREE STATES MUST HAVE LAID
    CLAIM
ON THAT HIDE THAT HAD GAINED SOME LITTLE FAME.
BUT NONE OF IT MADE ANY SENSE, AND THE
    INSPECTOR
SAYS "DON'T YOU SHIP, AND DON'T SLIP AND
    BUTCHER".

AND THE RAILROAD SEZ THEY GOT NO CLAIM
     PENDING
ON A COW - THEY JUST RUN TRAINS FOR A LIVING.
AND THE RANCH SEZ THEY FED THIS COW SEVEN
     YEARS,
AND THEY NEEDN'T HEAR THE NEAR NEIGHBOR'S
     JEERS.

ONCE MORE THE COW GOES TO FORAGE HILLSIDES,
THIS TIME WITHOUT HAVING A NEW CALF INSIDE.
AS A NEW HAND, I TRY TO FIGURE OUT HOW THIS WILL
WORK OUT -AND THE OLD HANDS SAY JUST TO BE
     STILL.

AND THEN ME AND THE FOREMAN GETS INTO A FIGHT
AND I GO TO TOWN WITH THE NEXT MORNING LIGHT.
AND I'LL BET SINCE THE WINTER WAS MIGHTY HARD,
COW OWNERSHIP WAS ARGUED BY COYOTE AND
     BUZZARD.

'CAUSE SHE DIDN'T BELONG TO THE RANCHER THAT
     FED HER
AND SHE COULDN'T MOVE ON 'TIL BRAND READIN' WAS
     BETTER.
THE INSPECTOR WAS WATCHIN' WHATEVER THEY'DE
     DO,
AND THE RAILROAD ONLY WANTED TO PUT THE TRAINS
     THROUGH.

---

*The neighbor's cows eat your grass in
proportion to how well you mend fence.*

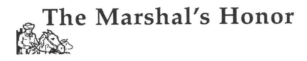# The Marshal's Honor

THE MARSHAL JUST PAID ME HONORS
THAT I'D NEVER KNOWN BEFORE.
IT MADE ME FEEL REAL GOOD INSIDE,
THAT BROAD SMILE THAT HE WORE.

HE PRAISED ME IN KNOWING TRAILS
THAT OTHER'S COULDN'T FIND.
AND HE SAID I WAS RIDING GOOD
TO GALLUP THROUGH THE PINES.

AND ON ACROSS THE SAGE LAND
WE HAD HURRIED WITHOUT REST,
WHEN NO ONE ELSE REALLY KNEW
WHETHER WE WERE EAST OR WEST.

HE SAID I'D DRINK FROM SINKHOLES
TOO MUDDY FOR A TOAD;
FIND A WAY PAST WILDERNESS
THAT WOULD NEVER KNOW A ROAD.

HE THOUGHT I WAS AWFUL GOOD
WITH A SHOOTIN' IRON AT NIGHT.
HE APPRECIATED MY CUNNING WAYS
WHILE FIGHTING WITHOUT LIGHT.

AND HE LIKED MY CHOICE OF HORSES,
AND MY SADDLE THAT WAS NEW.
AND THE BRIDLE AND THE BLANKET,
HE THOUGHT THEM PRETTY, TOO.

AND HE KNOWS THAT I'M INTELLIGENT
FOR A COMMON RANCHING HAND.
SO HE COULDN'T REALLY FIGURE
WHY I MISTOOK THAT BRAND.

AND HE DIDN'T LIKE BEING SNEAKY
TO COME UPON MY CAMP.
CAUSE IT <u>WAS</u> KINDA DARK LAST NIGHT
WITHOUT COOKING FIRE OR LAMP.

HE GAVE ME A FRESH HORSE TO SIT ON
FOR AN ENTHRALLING TRIP.
I'M SITTING HIGH AND MIGHTY
WHERE OTHER MEN HAVE SLIPPED.

HE GAVE ME A NEW HEMP NECKTIE
AND BY NOW YOU OUGHTA SEE,
HE'S GONNA WHIP THAT HORSE
AND LEAVE ME HANGING IN THE TREE!

The Killer

JOHN GOT A DROP ON THE DUDE
        WHO COULD ONLY THINK TO GRUNT.
HE COULDN'T HAVE HAD A BETTER CHANCE
        WITH A FULL STAKE-OUT HUNT.
HE CAUGHT HIM IN THE CORRAL,
        BOTHERING OLD JOHN'S FAVORITE ROAN.
HE WAS A BIT SURPRISED TO SEE HIM
        IN DAYLIGHT, SO CLOSE-IN TO HOME.
"THIS IS THE LAST YOU'LL BE SEEN,"
        SAYS JOHN, IN A LOWERED TONE,
"I BEEN WAITING FOR YOU TO APPEAR,
        AND I'M GLAD THAT YOU ARE ALONE.
FOR YOU, ROUNDS OF THE ENCIRCLING RANGE
        ARE FINISHED, STARTING RIGHT NOW.
YOU'LL SEE NO FLOWERS IN THE SPRING
        NOR NEW CALVES BESIDE THE COWS."
THE ONE AT BAY WAS 160 POUNDS OF NOTHING
        THAT WAS PRETTY TO SEE.
THROUGH PARTED LIPS HIS OFF-COLOR TONGUE
        HUNG LIKE A FLEXIBLE KEY.
STANDING IN HALF FROZEN MUD,
        HIS DIRTY BROW WORE A BIT OF A FROWN
HIS STANCE WAS THAT OF A CAUGHT-IN-THE-ACT,
        CHICKEN-EATING OLD HOUND.

THE ROAN IN DRIFTING APART,
        KEPT CLOSE WATCH ON THE SOLEMN AFFAIR.
WITH JOHN ACTING SO STRANGE,
        THE HORSE SMELLED BLOOD IN THE AIR.
WEATHER HAD AN AUTUMN COOL,
        THE GROUND HAD A LIGHT CASE OF SNOW,

THERE'D BE NO VISITORS 'TIL SPRING
AND NO ONE WOULD NEED TO KNOW.
JO ANNE, COMING DOWN FROM THE HOUSE,
DIDN'T LIKE WHAT SHE SAW;
SHE BEGGED JOHN TO BACK OFF, SETTLE,
UNTIL HIS COLD HEART COULD THAW.
SHE DIDN'T KNOW FOR SURE, AT THE MOMENT,
IF HE WAS ENTIRELY SANE,
AND SHE DIDN'T LIKE WATCHING
THE ACTIONS OF MALICE IN HIS BRAIN.
JOHN RANTED, " YOU MADE NEIGHBOR TROUBLE
AS YOU DOWNED THE BARBED WIRE FENCE,
NOW, YOU MADE ALL THE ILLS I'LL TAKE,
THERE'LL BE NO MORE OFFENSE.
YOU'VE BEEN EATING FROM MY TABLE,
AND YOUR POOR EXCUSES ALL ARE LAME.
IT IS SURE, YOU WON'T BUM NO MORE,
I'LL NOW BE ENDING ALL YOUR GAMES.

I'LL TAKE CARE AS I SHOOT YOU.
I THINK AFTER TANNING YOUR HIDE,
IT COULD MAKE A PRETTY PAIR OF GLOVES
WITH FAT SCRAPED OFF THE INSIDE.
THEN, MAYBE I SHOULD JIST BRAND YOUR HIDE,
SO EVERYONE KNOWS THAT YOU WERE MINE.
OR, YOU'D MAKE A FAIR GOOD WINDOW COVER
WHEN THE SNOW IS BLOWING REAL FINE."
THEN JOHN, CALM AS ANY MAN EVER IN CHURCH,
PULLED UP HIS RUSTY FORTY FIVE,
TOOK GOOD AIM; SHOT THAT TROUBLE MONGER
RIGHT BETWIXT THE EYES.
THE BODY DROPPED QUICK TO THE EARTH,
AND OF STUGGLING THERE WAS NONE.
JOHN HAD TAKEN HIS FULL REVENGE,
AND HAD KILLED THE SON OF A GUN.
"I'LL GET MY KNIFE AND BLEED HIM OUT,"
JOHN SAID, IN A STABLE VOICE,

AND THAT HE DID, TAKING MOST ALL DAY
    TO CUT HIM UP, OF COURSE.
JO ANNE HAD NOT EXPECTED BLOODY BUTCHERY
    IN THE CORRAL THAT DAY.
SHE HIDE HERSELF IN A SMALL BACK ROOM,
    AND KEPT FROM HER HUSBAND'S WAY.

THEN HE WENT AND TALKED CALMLY ON THE PHONE
    AND CONFESSED THE SORDID THING,
AND ORDERED ANOTHER LITTLE PIG
    TO RAISE ON HIS RANCH IN THE SPRING.

I Understand

I UNDERSTAND HOW HE WENT FOR THAT YOUNG GAL.
I THOUGHT A BIT KINDLY ABOUT HER MYSELF.
I UNDERSTAND THAT HE WAS TIRED OF RIDING
    BRONC'S
AND HAVING LITTLE VITTLES ON HIS SHELF.

I UNDERSTAND THAT WORKING SICK CATTLE EVERY
    SPRING
DON'T MAKE A MAN AT PEACE INSIDE.
I UNDERSTAND THAT THE RIDING LIFE DOESN'T OFFER
    MUCH,
AND BEING SEEN AS POOR HURT'S PRIDE.

I UNDERSTAND THAT GOD LOVES US EQUAL EVERY
    ONE
AND KNOWS THOUGHTS AND INTENT SOMEHOW.
BUT I DON'T UNDERSTAND WHAT IS IN JOHN'S MIND.
WHAT MAKES A MAN GO OUT AND BUY A PLOW?

Instructions to Milkers

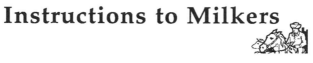

SOME COWS ARE MEAN WHEN IN THE STALL,
AND A Y-CROSS COW IS WORST OF ALL.
A LITTLE GRAIN MAY KEEP HER STILL,
BUT IF'N IT DON'T, NOTHING WILL.
USE THE HOBBLES, THEY'RE ON THE WALL;
LOCK THE STANCHION, AND LET HER BAWL.

THE PAIL MAY FLY, THE STOOL MAY BREAK,
WHEN PULLIN' TEATS HERE YOUR LIFE'S AT STAKE.
WHEN THE BUCKET'S FULL, STRAIGHTEN YOUR HAT,
STOP ROUND THE CORNER AND FEED THEM TWO CATS.
TURN THE OLD BIDDY OUT TO WATER AND GRASS,
IF SHE'S KINDA SLOW, FORGIVE THE OLD LASS.

DON'T CUSS HER, JIST LOVE HER, AND GIVE HER A PAT.
RANCHERS PAY BETTER FER THINGS DONE LIKE THAT.
SEPARATE WHAT MILK IS LEFT IN THE PAIL;
KEEP SELF AND UTENSILS CLEAN WITHOUT FAIL.
MILK NIGHTS FOR THE COOK, AND MORNS FOR THE BOSS.
REGULARITY OF TIME PREVENTS BUTTERFAT LOSS.

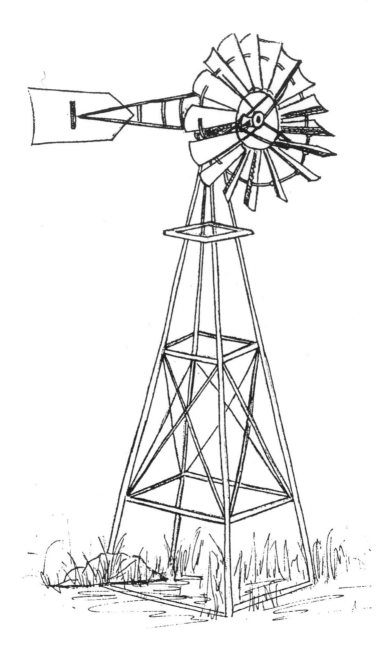

Changing Winds

THE FOREMAN SAID THE MILL NEEDED REPAIR
AND I WAS TO GIT THE JOB DONE.
HE SAID REPAIRING A WINDMILL IS EASY
AND I'D FIND IT TO BE LOTS OF FUN.

SO I HITCHED UP THE OLD SORREL TEAM
AND LOADED THE WAGON WITH TOOLS.
AND I STARTED OUT ACROSS GRASSLAND
WITHOUT REVIEWING SOME RULES.

I COULD SEE WHEN I PULLED UP AT THE MILL
THAT THIS WAS A JOB FOR A KID.
WHY WOULD HE SEND SUCH A GOOD MAN AS ME
TO DO MINOR CHORES, LIKE HE DID?

WELL, TIIIS WOULD BEAT A DAY'S RIDING;
I FIGURED TO BE HOME BY NOON.
THE OTHER BOYS WOULD BE OUT ALL DAY,
AND MAYBE RIDE HOME BY THE MOON.

SO, I STARTED RIGHT IN ASSESSING THE JOB
TO FIND OUT WHAT HAD TO BE DONE.
IN APPROACHING THE TASK I SOON FOUND
THAT THE LADDER WAS MISSING THREE RUNGS.

IT COULD BE EASY TO NAIL UP THE SLATS
STANDING ON THE WAGON FOR HEIGHT.
BUT THE TEAM MOVED ABOUT TERRIBLY FAST;
A SNAKE SCARED THE HORSE ON THE RIGHT!

I UNDERSTAND NOW JUST HOW HIGH UP
A FORTY FOOT DERRICK CAN STAND.
FROM HALF WAY UP I ALREADY COULD SEE
MUCH MORE THAN CONSIDERABLE LAND.

As I GAZED OUT AT THE BEAUTIFUL SIGHT
THE WRENCH SLIPPED OUT OF MY GRASP.
IN SCALING DOWN AND THEN QUICKLY BACK UP
I DISCOVERED THE NEST OF THE WASPS.

THEM PESKY BUGGERS HAD NEVER BEEN TOLD
THAT THE MILL WAS FOR USE OF A MAN.
AND THEY HAD HAD WATER, AND THEREFORE MUD,
TO BUILD HOMES THAT I WOULD HAVE BANNED.

PRAIRIE GRASS AND A MATCH FROM MY JEANS
MADE A TORCH THAT FIXED 'EM GOOD.
BUT THE SPARKS THAT JUMPED SURE DIDN'T
DO PRAIRIE GRASS ON THE GROUND ANY GOOD.

I AM CONSIDERABLE RESOURCEFUL.
I HAD A PAIL CLOSE, TO DIP IN THE TANK.
BUT THE MILL WAS BROKEN, REMEMBER,
AS THOUGH NATURE WAS PULLIN' A PRANK.

WELL, AN OLD FEED BAG DID WONDERS,
AS I BEAT THE FIRE FROM THE SOIL.
THE HORSES GOT TIED BACK TO THE MILL
AND I WEARILY RETURNED TO MY TOIL.

TIRED TIME IS NO TIME FOR CLIMBING
AND BY NOW I NEEDED SOME REST.
SO I FIGURED TO SIT ON THE PLATFORM
BUT THE WIND SHIFTED DIRECTLY TO WEST.

WHY DOESN'T A MILL SLOWLY ROTATE
TO MEET THE WIND IN ITS FACE,
INSTEAD OF SITTING SILENT, AND THEN
BRISKLY MOVING TO WHERE YOU'RE BRACED?

SURE, I DROPPED THAT OLD CRESCENT WRENCH.
YOU BET IT HIT THE HORSE ON THE RUMP.
BY THE TIME I GOT BACK UP ON THE MILL
I WISHED THE WHOLE THING TO THE DUMP.

THERE I SAT, MAD, HALF WAY TO HEAVEN
WITH A NERVOUS TEAM DOWN BELOW.
TIME WAS FAST WORKING AGAINST ME
WITH THE WIND BEGINNING TO BLOW.

I GOT A GOOD HOLD ON THE WRENCH THIS TIME
AND STRADDLED THE TAIL OF THAT MILL.
I ADJUSTED WRENCH SIZE, AND OPENED THE
GEAR BOX THAT WAITED TO BE FILLED.

THE OIL, OF COURSE, WAS AT THE BOTTOM
SITTING JIST BACK OF THE WAGON TONGUE .
DOWN I WENT, NOW WITH SOME PRACTICE,
AND BACK UP WITH TWO STRAINING LUNGS.

FOUR GALLONS OF OIL IS A BURDENSOME LOAD
FOR THE DRY ROTTED RUNGS OF A MILL,
BUT I GOT ON BY ON MY TRIP TO THE SKY
AND GAVE THAT GEAR BOX A FULL FILL.

IT WASN'T EASY TO FILL THAT OLD BOX
WITH NO FUNNEL TO FASHION THE FLOW.
SO, WHEN THE WIND SHIFTED OFF TO SOUTH,
I OILED EVERYTHING LOCATED BELOW.

IT DID MAKE THE STEPPING SOME SLIPPERY
AND I HAD TO HANG ONTO THE TAIL.
AT THAT, I SLID OUT OFF THE PLATFORM
STILL HOLDING THE HALF EMPTY PAIL.

I WAS OUT IN WESTERN SPACE, HANGING
IN A BREEZE THAT HAD WORKED UP TO STIFF.
I'D STILL BE THERE, I SURELY SWEAR,
IF THE WIND HADN'T TAKEN A SHIFT.

THIS IS WHEN I FOUND OUT ABOUT WINDMILLS
AND HOW THEIR TAIL CAN BE TURNED,
AND THE BLADES SLOWED DOWN FOR REPAIRS;
IT'S A WONDERFUL THING TO HAVE LEARNED.

HOWEVER, THE TAIL-WIRE ON THIS MILL WAS BUSTED
AND SOME TWINE WAS ALL I COULD USE
TO TIE THAT THING TIGHT FOR FURTHER REPAIR
WITHOUT MY BODY BEING FURTHER ABUSED.

THAT TOOK ANOTHER TRIP DOWN THE DERRICK
THROUGH THE OIL SLIME SPILL THAT I'D HAD.
BUT I TIED 'ER TIGHT TO HOLD ALRIGHT
AND IN SAFETY, I FELT NOT BAD.

DANG, IF IT WASN'T TOWARD NOON TIME
AND I'D NO GRUB IN BROWN SADDLE BAG.
I'D RATHER BEEN ON MY SADDLE HORSE
THAN WORKING WITH OLD OILY RAGS.

SO SETTLING FOR QUITTING AT MID-AFTERNOON
I WENT BACK TO WORK ON THE ROD.
A NEW STICK HAD TO BE WHITTLED TO FIT
BUT AT LEAST I COULD STAND ON THE SOD.

PULLING THAT SUCKER ROD UP BY MYSELF
WAS A CHORE FOR MEN TO BEHOLD.
I CAN DO ALMOST IMPOSSIBLE THINGS,
BUT THAT PULL ALMOST MADE ME FOLD.

STANDING IN THE HOT SUN BY THE WAGON,
THERE WAS JUST A POWDER UNDER MY FEET,
NOTHING BUT MUD IN THE WATER TANK,
AND I STILL HAD NOTHING TO EAT.

THE VALVE WAS JUST A MITE SMALLER
THAN LEATHERS BROUGHT FROM THE SHOP.
I TRIMMED 'EM DOWN AS BEST AS I COULD
TO HAVE REASONABLE FIT WHEN I STOPPED.

I DROPPED THE VALVE AND ROD IN THE HOLE,
HITCHED THE STICK ON TOP, JIST SUBLIME,
I WAS READY FOR HOME WHEN IT OCCURRED TO ME
THAT I HAD THE MILL TIED TIGHTLY WITH TWINE.

I WAS TEN RUNGS UP ON THAT SLICK DERRICK
WHEN THE FLYS GOT THE HORSE IN THE FLANK.
I WAS GLAD THE TETHER WAS REALLY TIGHT
WHEN THE SORREL JUMPED INTO THE TANK.

BACK DOWN I WENT TO STRAIGHTEN THE MESS,
TANK, HARNESS AND HORSES, AND WAGON.
I CONJURED UP PATIENCE THAT NO MAN HAD,
BY THE END, MY ENDURANCE WAS FLAGGIN'.

I GOT MYSELF PUSHED BACK UP ON THE DERRICK
AND GOT OUT MY TRUSTY OLD KNIFE.
I HEADED THE MILL TO THE WINDWARD,
AND GAVE THE TWINE A SOLID QUICK SLICE.

Wouldn't you know, a whirlwind of dry air
came from the ground with a blast.
Whipped that mill three quarters around,
and made me remember my past.

That fin-holdin' tail hit my belt line
and gave me an etheral thrill.
I caught it under my left arm pit.
On a hot day, my spine felt a chill.

I'm relatin' this record ain't I?
I managed to live through the ordeal.
But I want all riding hands to know
jist how it is that I feel.

The next time the foreman says "windmill,"
I'll check wind to south and south west.
And I will be headed north by north east
with my final pay in my vest.

---

*The fellow that says he never needs
help is always talking from the
middle of a crowd.*

Travel Advisory

ALWAYS RIDE TO TOWN WHEN THE WEATHER IS TOUGH,
WHEN IT'S SO BAD THAT THEY STOP THE MAIL.
MAKE SURE YOU HAVE THE WIND IN YOUR FACE;
IT'S GOOD IF IT'S PLUMB FULL OF HAIL.

ALWAYS HEAD OUT WHEN YOU'RE FACING A STORM,
NOT JUST CHINOOK OR A SQUALL, BUT A BLAST.
MAKE DOGGONE SURE IT'S A TEMPEST OF SORTS
AND NOT SOME SMALL GUST THAT WON'T LAST.

JUST YOU STAY PUT 'TIL A CYCLONE KICKS IN
AND IT COOLS THINGS TO UNSEASONAL FREEZE.
NEVER RIDE TO TOWN BUT AGAINST STRONG WIND
SO THAT COMING BACK HOME IS A BREEZE.

School

HE WAS A LITTLE OLDER THAN MOST BOYS STARTING
AT THE SCHOOL,
BUT HIS PARENTS WANTED LEARNIN' SO HE WOULDN'T
BE A FOOL.
THEY TAUGHT THEIR BEST, THOUGH THEY HADN'T
MUCH FOR MEANS,
AND ALL THEIR TIME WAS TAKEN UP IN EARNING BEEF
AND BEANS.
BUT HE WAS A CURIOUS LAD, AND HE WOULD EVEN
LEAVE HIS DOG,
IF IT MEANT HE'D GET TIME FOR READING PICTURE
CATALOGUES.
HIS MA AND PA SEARCHED FOR SUCCESSFUL WAYS
AND THINGS TO TEACH,
AND EFFORTS WERE EXTENDED TO PUT GOOD STUFF
WITHIN HIS REACH.
SO THE SCHOOL MARM KNEW, FROM THE NEIGHBOR
LADIES' IDLE TALK,
THAT SHE WOULD GET A STUDENT WHO WOULD READ
AND SELDOM TALK.
BUT SHE KNEW FROM FORMAL TRAINING THAT SHE
WOULD NEED ASSESS
JUST HOW WELL THE BOY HAD LEARNED, HOW WELL
HE HAD PROGRESSED.
THE FIRST DAY OF NOVEMBER, WHEN THE COWS WERE
GATHERED IN,
WAS HER DAY FOR STARTIN' SCHOOL, SO WINTER
LEARNIN' COULD BEGIN.
CLASS BEGAN UNRULY; THEY'D NOT MET SINCE APRIL
ONE LAST SPRING,
BUT SHE HAD WITS ABOUT HER AND KNEW WHAT
SCHOOL DAYS BRING.

WITH SLATES CLEANED AND READY, AND SLATE
    PENCILS HANDED OUT,
SHE DECIDED TO START EARLY TO SHOW WHAT
    LEARNIN' WAS ABOUT.
SHE WANTED SOME RETENTION OF THE THINGS SHE
    TAUGHT EACH DAY,
AND RECITATION OF THE LEARNIN' WAS THE
    DEMONSTRATION WAY.
SO, SHE ASKS THE THREE NEW KIDS TO STAND
    BEFORE THE CLASS,
AND TELL WHAT THEY'D LEARNED FROM HOME
    SCHOOLING OF THE PAST.
THE FIRST TWO RESPONDED WITH WHAT *THEY*
    THOUGHT WAS NOTABLE,
AND JUST AS SHE SUSPECTED, NOT A THING SHE'D
    TEACH IN SCHOOL.
SHE FELT SMUG, SELF ASSURED INSIDE, BUT SHE HAD
    LOST HER BET,
HE STEPS FORTH AND SPEAKS OUT LOUD; SAYS HE
    KNOWS THE ALPHABET!
OH, MY! SHE EXPECTED A SMART LAD, BUT THIS
    SHE'D NOT PREPARED,
SO SHE DECIDED TO ASSESS HIM, AND ASKED
    RECITAL, IF HE DARED.
SO HE STARTED IN, WITH A VOICE REAL STRONG THAT
    DIDN'T FALL.
HE WAS AS SELF ASSURED AS SHE, HE DIDN'T
    HESITATE AT ALL.
"A", HE SAYS, "B, AND C ", AND THEN IN A TONE
    ENTIRELY FREE
HE INTERJECTS WITHOUT A THOUGHT, " AND DRAGGIN'
    D".
SHE HAD A SEIZURE IN HER HEART THAT HER TONGUE
    COULD NOT CONFESS,
HE HAD STARTED OUT SO GOOD, HOW WOULD HE
    HANDLE ALL THE REST?

BUT THE STUDENTS WERE ALL QUIET AND RESPECTFUL
AS COULD BE,
SO SHE LET HIM CONTINUE ON, AS THE BRIGHTEST OF
THE THREE.
"E" CAME QUICK AND HE FOLLOWS WITH "FLYING F",
AND PAUSED AT "G",
"H" WAS STRONG, THEN "I BAR", AND A QUICK, "J
HANGIN' TREE".
"K", HE SAYS, " LEANIN' L", "BOXED M", AND "BROKEN
N",
"CIRCLE", "LAZY P"; "Q", "ROCKIN R"; WOULD HE MAKE
THE END?
HOW COULD HE HAVE LEARNED THIS, WHAT WAS
THERE SHE COULD DO?
IT WASN'T RIGHT TO STOP HIM, RECITIN' WHAT HE
THOUGHT HE KNEW.
"SQUEEZED S", PIERCED HER HURTING EAR, THEN,
"TUMBLING T".
"U", "NARROW V", "RUNNING W", HE RECITES AS EASY
AS CAN BE.
BY NOW HE KNOWS HE'S GOT IT WHIPPED, HE'LL GET
CLEAR TO THE END.
"X OVER DOT", " Y OPEN BOX".   HIS TRIUMPH
MESSAGE HE DID SEND
WHEN HE FINISHED LOUDLY, AND SURELY PLAIN, WITH
"FINALLY, Z".
THEN LOOKIN' TEACHER IN THE EYE HE ASKS, "AIN'T YA
PROUD O' ME?"
SHE WAS SPEECHLESS DUMB, SHE COULDN'T THINK OF
WHAT TO SAY.
SHE WOULDN'T SCOLD SO BIG A LAD, IN SCHOOL FOR
HIS FIRST DAY.
THE NEIGHBOR KIDS KNEW ALL ALONG HE COULD
LEARN TO BEAT THE BAND,
WITH NO BIBLE IN HIS HOME, HE LEARNED FROM THE
BOOK OF BRANDS!

Style

My PERSONAL STYLE OF BULL RIDING
IS SITTING QUIETLY ON THE FENCE.
I DON'T WIN ANY PRIZES THAT WAY,
BUT I USE A LOT OF GOOD SENSE.

My PERSONAL STYLE OF BULL RIDING:
COLA IN HAND, WATCHING THE STANDS.
I FEEL SAFE NOT BEING TIED ON
AND EASILY HEAR TUNES OF THE BAND.

COWARDICE IS THE REASON MY STYLE
IS SITTING QUIETLY ON THE FENCE.
I CAN'T HANDLE THE RIP AND ROAR
OF BEING THROWN HIGH IN SUSPENSE.

I RELAX COUNTING THE MONEY CROWDS PAY.
I'M RICH GIVING THEM SOMEWHERE TO SIT.
I DON'T WIN ANY PRIZES THAT WAY,
AND IT BOTHERS ME NEVER ONE WHIT.

I'M CONSIDERED A STICK-IN-THE-MUD
WHOSE NERVES JUST NEVER GO TENSE.
I DON'T RIDE AND I DON'T GIVE ADVICE,
BUT I USE A LOT OF GOOD SENSE.

---

*It is bad enough to stumble around in
the other fellow's darkness; there is
no need to blow out your own candle.*

Rough Rider

I SURELY LEARN QUICK, AND AT YOUNG AGE
I HAD LEARNED TO RIDE HORSES WELL.
STICKING A HORSE GOT TO BE SOME FUN
AND I GATHERED UP STORIES TO TELL.

SOON, I WAS RIDING THE ROUGHEST STOCK,
AND I RODE WITH THE SLIGHTEST FEARS,
DIDN'T WANT TO LOOK A HORSE IN THE EYE,
I YEARNED TO SEE THE BACK OF HIS EARS.

ON THE *T BAR W* I RODE "THE FRIEND",
A HORSE WHICH SHOWED SEVERAL SHADES.
HE'S GREY OUTSIDE, BLACK IN HIS HEART;
THERE WASN'T WHITE WHEN HE WAS MADE!

THE *CIRCLE J* OFFERED A CHALLENGING MOUNT
THAT THE BOYS REFERRED TO AS "TWISTER".
HE TURNED QUICK AND ROLLED OVER SOME;
A THRILLING RIDE HE WAS, MISTER.

RIDING WAS NEVER BEHIND GATES IN A PEN.
I WOULDN'T CONSENT TO RIDE FROM A CHUTE.
OUT IN THE MEADOW, OR ON UP THE HILL,
I RODE FREE AS THE DEER ON THE BUTTE.

MOVING AROUND TO SEE THE WORLD, I FOUND
"SATAN" ON THE *D BAR*, WITH FITTING NAME.
WHEN RIDING WAS DONE AND MAN WAS DOWN,
IT WAS NEVER THAT HORSE WHO WAS LAME.

I MADE IT TO A PLACE WITH RODEO STOCK,
WHERE THE HORSES WERE ALL KNOWN BY NUMBERS.
EXCEPT THE ONE ASSIGNED TO ME, OF COURSE,
WHICH SOMEHOW HAD GOT THE NAME "RUMBLER".

A HORSE'S NAME USUALLY TOLD YOU A BUNCH
ABOUT HOW PEOPLE VIEWED HIS DEMEANER.
"CYCLONE" AND "STORM" AND "TORNADO"
WERE IN THE CLASS WITH OLD "STEAMER".

BUT I WATCHED CLOSE FOR THE SUBTLE NAMES
OF "LADY", "SWEETHEART", "BEAUTY", AND SORTS.
SOME OF THOSE GALS COULD RATTLE YOUR BONES
AND SHAKE YOU RIGHT OUT OF YOUR SHORTS.

I NEVER TURNED DOWN A GOOD HEARTY RIDE.
I NEVER LOOKED FOR A HORSE THAT WAS SOFT.
AND AIN'T STOVE UP FROM RIDING ROUGH STOCK.
I'M THIS WAY FROM BEING BUCKED OFF!

---

*Don't go to battle when the king's
war horse corral is filled with
jackasses*

Meat Dishes

MEAT'S ALL THE SAME, DOMESTIC OR GAME
YOU CAN'T TELL RED MEAT APART.
THAT'S WHAT WAS SAID BY A MAN NOW DEAD,
A RANCH COOK TO THE DEPTHS OF HIS HEART.

DON WAS THE COOK, WITH NO RECIPE BOOK
JUST INTUITION AND SKILL.
HE WOULD BOIL, BAKE, OR ROAST THE TAKE,
HE DIDN'T CARE HOW IT WAS KILLED.

NOR DID HE CARE IF IT FOULED THE AIR
ODORS WERE FIXED WITH HIS SPICE
ASK WE DIDN'T DARE; HE DIDN'T SHARE
WHAT WAS PUT IN A DISH, LOOKING NICE.

BEING LAME ONE DAY, AT HOME I STAYED
TO FAVOR AN INJURED KNEE.
AND I SAW DON GO, WITH GAIT SO SLOW
TO THE CORRAL, SNEAKY AS HE COULD BE.

A GOAT HE TIED, TO POST NOT HIGH,
WITH SUMMER'S HEAT IT'S WORST.
NO FEED HE GAVE, NOR WATER TO STAVE
THE RAVISHES OF HUNGER AND THIRST.

HE RETURNED AGAIN TO ROUND CORRAL PEN
TO WHIP THE INNOCENT GOAT.
IT KNEES WENT WEAK, IT COULDN'T BLEAT,
THERE WAS BLOODY SWEAT ON ITS COAT.

HE FIXED A NOOSE BEFORE IT GOT LOOSE
AND HALF HUNG THE ANIMAL.
IT GASPED AND CHOKED. DON JUST SOAKED
THE SUN WHILE HE GROOMED HIS MULE.

THEN A NEW FACTOR, THE RED RANCH TRACTOR
BECAME A TOOL FOR THE MAN.
LEAD ROPE ON DRAWBAR, DON DROVE SO FAR
THAT THE POOR GOAT NO LONGER RAN.

HE SLIT THE THROAT OF THE DOWNED GOAT.
NOT WAITING FOR BLOOD TO YIELD,
DON WENT TO HIGH GEAR, CONFIRMED MY FEARS,
HE DRAGGED DEAD GOAT TO PLOWED FIELD.

HE OPENED GOAT UP, STRUNG THE ANIMAL GUT
IN A FURROW GRAVE ON SOUTH SIDE.
WITH OPEN CARCASS BEHIND, HE DROVE BLIND
UNTIL THE ABUSED SKIN BEGAN TO SLIDE.

THEN BACK TO RANCH, AND ON A LOW BRANCH
THE GOAT WAS HUNG IN THE HEAT.
PUPS PLAYED AROUND, REACHIN' FROM GROUND
TO THE DEAD BODY FOR SOMETHING TO EAT.

I COULDN'T TAKE MORE, I CLOSED THE DOOR
OF THE BUNKHOUSE, LAID ON MY BED.
WHEN FOREMAN WAS BACK, I'D GET OFF MY SACK.
I KNEW WHAT WOULD HAVE TO BE SAID.

BUT INSTEAD OF COMING AROUND HE WENT TO TOWN
WHEN THE BOYS CAME TO THE TABLE.
I DIDN'T FEEL WELL WHEN DON RANG DINNER BELL
BUT I WOULD HAVE TO EAT TO STAY ABLE.

THE MEAL WAS GOOD, DON DID MAKE FINE FOOD
I FELT BETTER WITH BELLY FULL.
I TOOK SOFT APPROACH, AND WITHOUT REPROACH
ASK IF HE'D RATHER COOK MUTTON OR BULL.

MEAT'S ALL THE SAME, DOMESTIC OR GAME
YOU CAN'T TELL RED MEAT APART.
THAT'S WHAT WAS SAID BY A MAN NOW DEAD,
A RANCH COOK TO THE DEPTHS OF HIS HEART.

THEN I COULD SEE THAT IN THE LOW TREE
NO CARCASS HUNG IN SUNSET.
HAD THAT OLD GOAT PASSED THROUGH MY THROAT
WAS IT REALLY WHAT I HAD 'ET?

DON SAYS, "LIKE TODAY, IN COOKING I SLAVED,
YOU HAVE UNDERSTANDING, I HOPE,
IT TAKES LOTS OF TIME, TO FIX MEALS SUBLIME
LIKE THIS EVENINGS ANTELOPE."

People go to the funeral of the town
tyrant, but they don't cry.

Nine O'Clock

AT NINE O'CLOCK IN THE EVENING
ALL THE WORLD IS LEAVIN' HOME.
LOVERS SNEAK TO QUIET LANE,
HOT RODS OUT TO ROAM.

COUPLES GO TO MOVIES,
THE BOYS DRIFT TO A BAR.
THE GIRLS ROAM WINDOW SHOPPIN',
BE IT NEAR OR VERY FAR.

IT'S JUST THE START OF AN EVENING,
I HAVE HEARD IT SAID,
AT NINE O'CLOCK IN THE EVENING,
WHEN TIRED COWBOYS GO TO BED!

Gold!!

IT WAS A RIDING HAND'S DREAM COMING TRUE.
I WAS GONNA BE RICH; MY WORKING WAS THROUGH.
I HAD TROTTED TO WATER FOR MY THIRSTY STEED
AND FOUND GOLD LAYING IN THAT TANK. INDEED!
IT FLASHED, JUST SURE AS I'M TALKING TO YOU,
AND IT CERTAINLY REFLECTED A BEAUTIFUL HUE.

THE HORSE SHOOK HIS MUZZLE AS DEEPLY HE DRANK;
THE GOLD TOWARD THE BOTTOM SETTLED AND SANK.
BUT I UNDERSTOOD IT WAS THERE IN THE SLIME
AND GETTING IT OUT WOULD ONLY TAKE TIME.
I'D DRAIN THE BIG TANK IF THAT WAS REQUIRED
TO SEPARATE METAL FROM ANKLE-DEEP MIRE.

COULD YOU IMAGINE THE THING AT MY HAND?
A WINDMILL PUMPING GOLD FROM UNDER THE LAND!
I HAD ONLY TO INSTALL A PERMANENT SIEVE
TO REAP THE REWARDS WHICH WINDMILL WOULD GIVE.
BUT I DIDN'T REJOICE OR YELL AT THE TIME,
NO! I WANTED PROOF OF REWARD FROM THE SLIME.

SO I QUIETLY WENT ABOUT MY WORK FOR THE DAY,
BUT MY MIND COULDN'T SETTLE ON PUTTING UP HAY.
THEN IN THE EVENING I LEFT FROM THE TABLE
AND SAUNTERED APART AS SLOW AS I WAS ABLE,
AND I SHOVED MY HAND DEEP IN PROMISING WATER,
AND CONJURED UP BUYING INSTEAD OF BEEF BARTER.

IT WAS THERE! I SAW A FLECK AT THE OTHER END
THAT MADE MY MIND JUMP, AND JIGGLE, AND BEND.
GAD! CAN YOU UNDERSTAND WHAT WAS WITHIN GRASP
OF MY HAND; MY HEART SKIPPED, BREATH WAS A
    GASP.
I RAN TO THE SHED AND GRABBED UP A BIG SCOOP
THAT WE USED TO CLEAN OUT THE OLD CHICKEN
    COOP.

THEN I SLOWED, SO AS NOT TO HAVE ATTENTION
AS I SLOGGED WATER AND TOOK A GOOD DRENCHING.
I STOPPED WHEN THE WATER WAS TWO INCHES DEEP
SO I COULD WASH THE GOLD BEFORE I WOULD SLEEP.
BUT THE SLIME WAS STILL BENEATH THE COLD FLUID,
WAITING FOR MUCKING. I HAD TO SHOW I COULD DO
    IT.

LONG, I FINGERED THE GOO TO DISCOVER THE
    NUGGETS,
SO AS NOT TO THROW FORTUNES BY SCOOPING OR
    BUCKET.
I COULDN'T FIND 'EM, BUT I KNEW THEY WERE THERE,
I'D SEEN 'EM BY GOLLY, OR CATS DON'T GROW HAIR.
LUCK WAS ON MY SIDE AND THE MOONLIGHT
    APPEARED;
I'D WORK THROUGH THE NIGHT, THE SKY BEING
    CLEAR.

BY NOW, I STOOD INSIDE OF THE WATERING TANK
WITH SHIVERING BONES AND SMELLING SOME RANK.
I QUIT FOR A REST AND TO LET SLIMY MUCK SETTLE
BEFORE I'D GO BACK TO RECOVERING THE METAL.
THIS WOULD BE THE BEST DAWN THAT I'D EVER SEEN
ONCE I RAN THAT SLUDGE THROUGH A SMALL SCREEN.

JUST AFTER MIDNIGHT I REALLY TACKLED THE CHORE
I HAD RESTED A BIT AND WAS READY FOR MORE.
NERVES WERE SOME FRAYED, AND HARD TO CONTROL
IN THOUGHTS OF THE FORTUNE SO CLOSE IN THAT
    HOLE.
AND THEN I SAW A FLASH AND A FLECK SLIP AGAIN,
UP TO THE SURFACE, AND BACK DOWN WHERE IT'D
    BEEN.

WHAT A TEMPTATION IT WAS TO SPLASH AND TO
    FLAIL,
BUT I HELD TOGETHER SO NO EFFORTS COULD FAIL.
I SHOVED THE SCREEN OVER THAT WAY JUST A WEE
    BIT.
IF GOLD WAS TO MOVE, I'D HAVE A STRAINER ON IT.
IT TOOK THIRTY MINUTES TO GET ONE HELD IN HAND.
OH, COLOR AND RAPTURE; I DANCED ON THE LAND.

BUT IT DIDN'T HOLD STILL. THIS STUFF WAS ALIVE.
HAD I GONE PLUMB LOCO? DOES NATURE CONNIVE ?
WHEN I COME TO WATER, I DON'T EXCITE ANY MORE.
THAT GOLD WAS FISH MY KID GOT AT THE STORE.

---

*A man ain't always right when he is
rich, but being right feels like gold.*

The True Hand

HE KICKED HIS OWN BEHINDER.
HE FIGURED HE JUST COULDN'T THINK.
HE CURSED HIS LUCK, CLAIMED NO PLUCK,
AND ALMOST TURNED TO STRONG DRINK.

THERE WASN'T NO WAY THINGS COULD BE THIS BAD
SHAME WAS UPON HIM FOR CHOOSING SO WRONG
THERE WASN'T NO REASON FOR SUCH PLIGHT TO BE HAD,
BUT IT STUCK REAL TIGHT FOR HIS STAYING SO LONG.

THE WEIGHT WAS THE SAME FOR THE HANDLING,
THE DISTANCE FROM HERE TO WHENCE,
THOUGH IT SEEMED TO BE TEN TIMES LONGER,
WAS MEASURED EXACTLY BY THE SAME BARBED FENCE.

BUT THERE WASN'T NO FUN IN THE WORKING.
HE SOLD HIS SOUL FOR AN HOURLY DIME.
THE WAGES WERE REGULAR AND THE KITCHEN GOOD
BUT THE WORKING SEEMED TO TAKE TWICE THE TIME.

TALKIN TO FOLKS SHOWED THE SHORTNESS OF EARS.
A LITTLE OF LISTENIN' MADE A LOT OF TALK
AND THEN SOME THINGS GOT TO DOIN'
WHEN MAYBE THEY NEEDED A BALK.

HE FELT LIKE HE'D BEEN LEFT IN A GULLY,
AND THE REMOTE ROADS WEREN'T THE SAME,
MECHANIC'S STUFF COULDN'T STIR HIM
AND HE THOUGHT ALL OF LIFE TO BE LAME.

HE HANKERED TO BE KICKED BY HIS PARTNER.
HE FIGURED HE HAD JOINED UP WITH FOOLS,
CAUSE HE ENLISTED HISSELF IN AN OUTFIT
THAT PACKED UP IN TRUCKS INSTEAD O' MULES.

The Young Hand

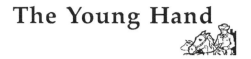

THE YOUNG HAND DOWN THE ROAD A PIECE
HAS SKILLS NOT FAR ADVANCED.
HE'S SO NERVOUS ON A BUCKIN' BRONC
THAT HE SOMETIMES WETS HIS PANTS.

A ROPE GETS TANGLED ON HIS SPURS
AND HIS HAT IS IN THE WAY.
I SAW HIM MOUNTING ALL ALONE-
FROM A FENCE- THE OTHER DAY.

HE'S GOT NO STRENGTH TO TOSS A BALE
NOR PULL A CALF IN SPRING.
HE CAN'T TIGHTEN UP A FENCE
NOR WORK ALONE FOR ANYTHING.

BUT GIVE HIM JUST A FEW MORE YEARS
AND HE'LL BE A COWBOY BOLD.
FOR THAT YOUNG HAND AT THE NEIGHBOR'S
IS MY GRANDSON, FOUR YEARS OLD.

Lonesome Cowboy

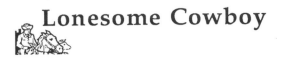

I AM HEADED TO THE CITY SO I CAN BE ALONE.
I HAVE TIRED OF THE ATTENTION I GET AT HOME.

THE COW NEEDS MILKING MORNING AND NIGHT.
WITHOUT WEEDING, THE GARDEN IS A FRIGHT.
HORSES WANT SHOEING, A CALF LACKS A BRAND,
THE SOW FARROWED PIGS TO BE BOTTLED BY HAND,
CHICKENS CACKLE THROUGH A FOX THREAT AT NIGHT,
THE HAY MEADOW HASN'T AS MUCH WATER AS IT
    MIGHT.
EVERYTHING TUGS AT ME THREE WAYS EVERY DAY,
'TIL EVENING DARKNESS MAKES ME HIT THE HAY.

I COME FROM THE CITY AND I KNOW ABOUT BUSTLE,
AND HOW THE PEOPLE THERE DISPLAY THEIR HUSTLE.
COOK HOUSES ON RANCHES ARE RIGHT FRIENDLY
    PLACES,
BUT TOWN WAITRESSES REMEMBER DOLLARS, NOT
    FACES.
I COULD GO TO BE IGNORED IN ANY TWO-BIT CAFE,
EVEN GIVING AN ORDER, THEY DON'T CARE WHAT I'D
    SAY.

MY RANCH IS RIGHT GOOD SIZE FOR A ONE MAN
    SHOW,
BUT I GET LOST IN THE LIBRARY EVERY TIME I GO.
THERE ARE ALLEYS AND AISLES NO END, IF YOU
    PLEASE,
ASK A QUESTION; THEY SAY "PUNCH THE COMPUTER
    KEYS."
I CAN FIND A THOUSAND COWS SCATTERED OVER MY
    LAND,

SEE ME AT THEIR DESK, BE DAD-GUMMED IF THEY CAN!
WALKING AROUND UNNOTICED IS NO SIGNIFICANT
    LABOR,
TOWN FOLKS WOULDN'T KNOW IF I WAS THEIR NEXT
    DOOR NEIGHBOR
MY NEIGHBOR AT HOME WILL WASTE A GOOD HALF A
    DAY
JUST ASKING ABOUT THE BUGS HE CAN SEE IN MY HAY.
BUT IN TOWN I CAN BE STRANDED FOR OVER A WEEK
AND I WON'T HAVE INTEREST FROM ONE OF THOSE
    GEEKS.

IN TOWN I'M AVOIDED LIKE THE PLAGUE IF I COUGH,
AT HOME HOGS GREET ME NO-MATTER AT THE TROUGH.
ONE'S NEVER BEEN COLD-SHOULDERED 'TIL YOUR OWN
CHURCH PEOPLE BRUSH BY IN THEIR HURRY FOR HOME.
EACH WEEK THE PASTOR HAS 'EM SHAKE, 'N SAY HELLO;
NEXT WEEK THEY'RE STILL STRANGERS, DON'T YA KNOW.
NOW LIQUID REFRESHMENT IS AN INTERESTING THING,
AROUND WHICH PEOPLE GATHER AND CHAT AND SING.
IN TOWN, THOSE HEIFERS JUST KEEP ON DRINKING,
THE COWS AT HOME WOULD HEAR WHAT I WAS THINKIN'.
I GUESS IN TOWN THERE JUST ISN'T MUCH TO SAY,
IF YOU HAVEN'T ANY CHORES AND YOU SIT ALL DAY.

THE HOTEL PEOPLE NEVER CARE IF I USE THE ROOM;
THEY STILL TIDY UP AND PUSH THEIR LITTLE BROOM.
BUT THEY HAVE INTEREST KEEN EVERY COUPLE DAYS
ABOUT THE BALANCE DUE, AND HOW IT WILL GET PAID.
SOMEHOW, IN THE CITY THEY NEVER GET BEDDED
    DOWN.
SEEMS THERE IS ALWAYS SOMEONE RAMMIN' AROUND.
THEY SEEM PLUMB SCARED, KEEP THE COPS ALERT.
THEY DON'T SLEEP ENOUGH; EVERY ONE IS CURT.

I AM HEADED TO THE CITY SO I CAN BE ALONE,
I HAVE TIRED OF THE ATTENTION I GET AT HOME.

Old Blue of the Terry Ranch

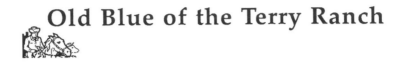

THERE'S A ROCKY GRAVE ON THE TERRY
THAT HAS QUITE A STORY TO TELL
OF A HORSE AND HIS RIDERS,
OF EXPLOITS ONLY HARD MEN KNOW WELL.
OLD BLUE WAS THE HERO SO BURIED,
THE BEST OF HORSES WITH ROPE,
THE FINEST AT CUTTIN' THE CATTLE,
AND SMOOTH AT BOTH TROT AND THE LOPE.
    WHERE EVER WE GO, WHAT EVER WE DO,
    WE CAN'T FORGET THE HORSE CALLED OLD BLUE.

SEEMS THIS HORSE COULD DO WONDERS,
THINGS BEYOND THE REALM OF A BEAST.
HE PROVIDED THE WEALTH OF THE RANCHER
AND STORIES OF BOASTIN' AT FEASTS.
OLD BLUE WAS REALLY QUITE SPECIAL,

BUT I CAN'T RELATE JIST HOW MUCH.
I NEVER LAID EYES ON THE FELLER;
I JIST HEARD STORIES AND SUCH.
>WHERE EVER WE GO, WHAT EVER WE DO,
>WE CAN'T FORGET THE HORSE CALLED OLD BLUE.

No MAN HAVE I MET THAT HAD RODE HIM
THOUGH SOME CLAIM THEY SAW IT DONE.
IT WASN'T BECAUSE HE WAS OUTLAW,
BUT CAUSE THE HONORS HAD TO BE WON.
MEN AT THE TERRY WERE FIGHTERS,
AND THEY'D FISTFIGHT ALL THROUGH THE NIGHT
TO BE THE BEST MAN IN THE MORNING
TO MOUNT BLUE WHEN DAWN SHOWED SOME LIGHT.
>WHERE EVER WE GO, WHAT EVER WE DO,
>WE CAN'T FORGET THE HORSE CALLED OLD BLUE.

BLUE WAS SO GOOD UNDER SADDLE
THAT A MAN COULD REST THROUGH THE DAY,
'CAUSE THAT HORSE WOULD DO ALL THE WORKIN'
AND THE COWBOY DREW ALL THE PAY.
A PILE OF BROKE ROPE IN THE BUNKHOUSE
HAD BEEN TIED TO BLUE'S SADDLE SOME TIME;
BUT IT WASN'T AS STRONG AS THAT PONY
WHEN HE STOPPED YEARLIN' STEERS ON A DIME.
>WHERE EVER WE GO, WHAT EVER WE DO,
>WE CAN'T FORGET THE HORSE CALLED OLD BLUE.

HE HAD SENSE BEYOND ANY MASTER,
SKILLS BEYOND THOSE THAT ARE TAUGHT.
HE DESERVED THE BEST GRAIN AND GRAZIN',
HIS TACK WAS THE BEST TO BE BOUGHT.
THAT HORSE KNEW WHERE COWS HID IN SUMMER,
WHERE CALVES WERE SPIRITED AWAY.
HE KNEW BRANDS OF SIX NEIGHBOR RANCHES,
AND WHERE WORK WAS LINED OUT EACH DAY.
>WHERE EVER WE GO, WHAT EVER WE DO,
>WE CAN'T FORGET THE HORSE CALLED OLD BLUE.

No HAND EVER CUSSED HIM AS ORNERY.
HE WAS GENTLE WITH KIDS AND THE WIFE.
NO REINS, HACK, OR BRIDLE WERE NEEDED.
HE KNEW WHERE TO BE ALL HIS LIFE.
BLUE NEVER HAD HIS LEGS HOBBLED,
NEVER FELT FETTER OR ANY RESTRAINT,
NATURALLY STAYED IN CLOSE FOR WORKIN'.
HE WAS TRUSTED AS MUCH AS A SAINT.
      WHERE EVER WE GO, WHAT EVER WE DO,
      WE CAN'T FORGET THE HORSE CALLED OLD BLUE.

No ONE WASTED TIME TRAININ',
NO TACK WAS TORN THROUGH OR TORN.
THAT HORSE DIDN'T NEED TO BE BROKEN,
HE WAS A WORKER FROM WHEN HE WAS BORN.
AT BRANDIN', HE WAS QUICK AND REAL QUIET.
THE CALVES SETTLED DOWN AS HE CAME,
HE LET YOUNG HANDS LEARN THEIR ROPIN';
STOOD STILL WHEN HEMP CAUGHT IN HIS MANE.
      WHERE EVER WE GO, WHAT EVER WE DO,
      WE CAN'T FORGET THE HORSE CALLED OLD BLUE.

HE COULD SENSE WHEN HORN-FLIES WERE RAMPANT
BUT HE NEVER TAIL-SWATTED A THING
IF IT MIGHT UPSET A DOGIE
OR ANY UNHAPPINESS BRING.
OLD BLUE COULD BE RODE ON FOREVER
WITHOUT STOP FOR DRINK OR FOR REST.
HE HAD NEVER BEEN TIRED BEYOND WORKIN'
AND WOULD SNICKER AT THE LEAST LITTLE JEST.
      WHERE EVER WE GO, WHAT EVER WE DO,
      WE CAN'T FORGET THE HORSE CALLED OLD BLUE.

POLITE HE WAS AT THE WATER..
LETTING OTHERS HAVE THEIR FULL FILL
BEFORE HE SIPPED UP HIS LIQUID
AND RETURNED TO WORK WITH A WILL.
HE WANTED TO PLEASE AND BE FAITHFUL

MORE THAN EVEN THE NEWEST OF BRIDES.
IF ANYONE SAID AUGHT ABOUT HIM,
IT WASN'T 'CAUSE HE HADN'T TRIED.
　　WHERE EVER WE GO, WHAT EVER WE DO,
　　WE CAN'T FORGET THE HORSE CALLED OLD BLUE.

THAT HORSE HAD A HIDE THAT WAS LOVELY.
IT SHONE A LUXURIOUS BLUE,
THE PRIDE OF HIS OWNER AT FAIR TIME
AS FOLKS ADMIRED TEXTURE AND HUE.
MEN SAT AT THE TABLE AND MARVELED
AT HOW THAT OLD HORSE COULD COMPETE,
FOR ANIMALS MANY YEARS YOUNGER
HADN'T HALF THE SPEED WITH THEIR FEET.
　　WHERE EVER WE GO, WHAT EVER WE DO,
　　WE CAN'T FORGET THE HORSE CALLED OLD BLUE.

WHEN BLUE'S COLTS ROMPED IN THE MEADOW
GOOD MEN WOULD STAND AND ADMIRE
THE APPEALING PROSPECTS OF PROFIT,
FOR EACH SON HAD THE TRAITS OF HIS SIRE.
UNDERSTAND, THE WORTH OF THAT HORSEFLESH
AND THE REASONS THE STORIES ARE TOLD
ARE SO TRUTHFULLY GREAT AND SO MANY
THAT THEY WILL ALWAYS UNFOLD.
　　WHERE EVER WE GO, WHAT EVER WE DO,
　　WE CAN'T FORGET THE HORSE CALLED OLD BLUE.

ONE CAN REGALE OF BLUE BY THE HOUR
ONE CAN RECALL THE STORIES OF OLD
ONE CAN BEST JUST STAND BY IN WONDER
AT HOW MUCH OCCURRED THAT HASN'T BEEN TOLD.
IF YOU GET OFF ON VACATION
AND PASS BY THE TERRY, I HOPE
YOU'LL TIP YOUR HAT TO THE GRAVE SITE
OF THE BEST THAT EVER PULLED ON A ROPE.
　　WHERE EVER WE GO, WHAT EVER WE DO,
　　WE CAN'T FORGET THE HORSE CALLED OLD BLUE.

A Man From Chicken Springs

A MAN RODE IN FROM CHICKEN SPRINGS
WHO LOOKED AS HARD AS THE RIDE.
A TACITURN MAN WITH A LEATHERY TAN
AND A RIFLE CLOSE AT HIS SIDE.

TOBACCO CRATERED DUST WHEREVER HE SPAT
WITHOUT RESPECT TO THE SCENE.
OLD BUCKSKIN CLOTHES, HIDES OF THREE DOES,
TOLD OF A MAN...WELL, UNCLEAN.

HIS RANGE-BRED MOUNT WAS SURE NERVOUS
AND SHIFTED IT'S EYES BACK AND FORTH.
THE TAIL SWITCHED AND EARS TWITCHED
AT NOISES STRANGE TO THE HORSE.

THE MAN HAD STARTED IN BEFORE DAYBREAK
AND NOW IT WAS LONG PAST MIDDAY.
HE HAD ONE JOB TO DO. THEN HE'D BE THROUGH
AND HOPEFULLY GO ON HIS WAY.

HE WENT DIRECT TO THE MERCHANT'S
AND THREW GOLD COIN ON THE BOARD,
THEN, HINTING A SMILE, TOOK A BAG FROM A PILE
AND SHOULDERED IT OUT THROUGH THE DOOR.

WITH THE BAG THROWN BACK OF THE SADDLE
AND TETHERED WITH RAWHIDE STRANDS,
HE TIGHTENED THE GIRTH AND SPRANG FROM EARTH
TO THE SADDLE WITH REINS IN HIS HANDS.

HE NEVER LOOKED BACK AT THE SETTLERS
WHO STARED IN AWE IN THE HEAT.
KNEES SQUEEZED COMMAND TO HORSE FROM THE MAN
AND THEY SILENTLY MOVED DOWN THE STREET.

HE WENT OUT THE WAY OF HIS COMING
AND NEVER AGAIN HAS BEEN SEEN.
ALL HE DESIRED WAS WHAT LIFE REQUIRED,
A NEW SUPPLY OF DRIED BEANS.

Full Menu

A NEW COOK WAS HIRED TO KEEP US IN VITTLES,
WHO MADE DIFFERENT USE OF SKILLETS AND
    KETTLES.
THAT COOK HAD BEEN <u>SOMEWHERE</u> TO LEARN ALL
    THIS STUFF
THAT HAD STRANGE SPICES, AND SAUCES, AND FLUFF.
RECIPES WERE USED THAT NOT ONE OF US DREAMED;
MORE FANCY EACH SERVIN', EACH DAY, SO IT SEEMED.
WE SUDDENLY HAD FLUFFY, SWEET WAFFLES FOR
    LUNCH,
AND QUAINT LITTLE PASTRIES ON SUNDAY FOR
    BRUNCH.
FRESH BEANS WERE CUT AND STEAMED 'STEAD O'
    BOILED,
AND BEEF MARINATED WAS SAUTED IN FRESH OLIVE
    OIL.
IT WAS SURE STRANGE WHEN THEY SERVED UP THE
    STRUDEL,
BUT IT TASTED AS GOOD AS THE RICH, SPICY
    NOODLES.
CORN HAD PIMENTOS, SPAGHETTI HAD BIG CHUNKS OF
    STEAK,
THERE WAS SOUR CREAM SAUCES, AND ICE CREAM
    AND CAKE.
IN THE EVENINGS CAME BON-BONS AND OTHER FINE
    CANDY,
AND POPCORN, AND SOFT DRINKS, AND PRETZELS
    WERE HANDY.

A COOK HOUSE HAD NEVER BEEN INVITING LIKE
    THIS.
WE HAD JUST BEEN EATING; THE DINING WAS MISSED.
THE FLOOR WAS SLEPT CLEAN QUICK AFTER EACH
    MEAL;
CLOTHS ON THE TABLE OF PROPER SETTING SHOWED
    ZEAL.
OUT WENT THE BOARDS WE HAD BEEN USING FOR
    SEATS
AND UP WENT CURTAINS WITH COLOR, PRESSED NEAT.
PADDED CHAIRS WERE COMFY AT THE END OF LONG
    DAYS,
AND WALL HANGINGS SETTLED NERVES IN NEW WAYS.
ONE DAY THE FOREMAN COMES HOME FROM PAYING
    THE VET
AND FELT HE NEEDED PRODUCTION IN LINE WITH THE
    DEBT.
AND THE GOOD WOMAN GOT FIRED, AND WE GOT A
    MAN COOK,
AND ALL WENT BACK TO BEEF AND BEANS, AND OLD
    LOOKS.

---

*Cream risen to the top will spoil if it
ain't used.*

Leghorn

MY DAD WAS RAISED ON A FARM; HE COULDN'T
    LEAVE THE SOIL,
AND WHEN WE MOVED TO TOWN HE WISHED TO
    CONTINUE HIS TOIL.
HE BOUGHT A SMALL PLOT ON THE EXTREME EDGE OF
    THE BURG
WHERE HE HAD A COW, HORSE, SWINE, AND PLANTS
    TO EMERGE.
I LEARNED TO HARNESS, RIDE, MILK, FEED AND THE
    LIKE
BUT THERE WERE A FEW QUESTIONS IN THE MIND OF
    THIS TYKE.
      MY DAD WAS AN OLD FARMER, AND HE'D KNOW
      WHAT TO DO.
      I'D GET HIS ADVICE AND THEN SEE THE THING
      THROUGH.

WE HAD AN OLD BUILDING THAT WASN'T BEING USED
    VERY MUCH\
IN THERE WE JUST STORED WORN TOOLS, AND HOSES,
    AND SUCH.
DAD THOUGHT IT A CHANCE TO TEACH SOME THINGS
    TO SONNY,
IF HE COULD INHABIT THAT SHED WITH STOCK
    EARNING MONEY.
I MIGHT HAVE TO HAVE HELP WHERE I REALLY DIDN'T
    KNOW.
BUT HE COULD HELP DIRECT WHERE AND HOW IT
    WOULD GO.
      MY DAD WAS AN OLD FARMER, AND HE'D KNOW
      WHAT TO DO.
      I'D GET HIS ADVICE AND THEN SEE THE THING
      THROUGH.

WELL, HE BOUGHT LEGHORNS, ACTUALLY FIVE
    HUNDRED CHICKS,
AND IT DIDN'T TAKE LONG TILL I WAS IN A SMALL FIX.
THOSE CHICKS NEEDED WARMTH EVERY MOMENT
    DURING SPRING
AND THEY PILED UP AND SMOTHERED AT THE LEAST
    THING.
I MUST HAVE BEEN ROUGH THAT DAY AS I PULLED
    THEM APART.
I KNOW I REALIZED THAT THE PROJECT HAD A ROUGH
    START.
    MY DAD WAS AN OLD FARMER, AND HE'D KNOW
    WHAT TO DO.
    I'D GET HIS ADVICE AND THEN SEE THE THING
    THROUGH.

THOSE CHICKS HAD A NICE FUNERAL, THOUGH IN A
    MASS GRAVE
BECAUSE DOING IT QUICK WAS THE ADVICE THAT HE
    GAVE.
THE OTHER CHICKS GREW TOGETHER, GOT FEATHERS
    ON WINGS.
EXCEPT ONE WAS BIGGER AND TOOK THE ATTITUDE OF
    A KING.
IT HELD IT'S HEAD VERY HIGH, AND MADE A STRANGE
    NOISE
AND IT STRUTTED AND BULLIED, AND ALWAYS ACTED
    ANNOYED.
    MY DAD WAS AN OLD FARMER, AND HE'D KNOW
    WHAT TO DO.
    I'D GET HIS ADVICE AND THEN SEE THE THING
    THROUGH.

"WHY, SON", HE SAID, "THAT CHICKEN IS A
    ROOSTER, A COCK.
EVERY FARMER NEEDS ONE TO BUILD AND IMPROVE
    HIS FLOCK."

BUT HE DIDN'T SAY HOW THAT THE BIRD WOULD BE
      POSSESSIVE;
IF CHALLENGED FOR HENS COULD GET DOWNRIGHT
      AGGRESSIVE.
THAT BIRD BEGAN WITH JUST A SMALL PECK ON MY
      SMALL LEG
AND THEN HE PROGRESSED UNTIL FOR AN END I
      WOULD BEG.
      MY DAD WAS AN OLD FARMER, AND HE'D KNOW
      WHAT TO DO.
      I'D GET HIS ADVICE AND THEN SEE THE THING
      THROUGH.

WHY, PSHAW," HE SAID, "THERE WAS NEVER IN
      HISTORY A TIME
WHEN A ROOSTER COULD BRING HARM TO A SMALL
      SON OF MINE."
HE MEANT FOR ME TO IGNORE THAT GROWING COCK
      AND HIS ANTICS,
BUT THE BIRD BECAME STRONGER AND DROVE ME
      CLEAR FRANTIC.
HE WOULD BEAT ME WITH STRONG WINGS, AND PECK,
      AND CLAW,
AND CHASE ME THROUGH THE BARNYARD, AND TO
      CRYING FOR MA.
      MY DAD WAS AN OLD FARMER, AND HE'D KNOW
      WHAT TO DO.
      I'D GET HIS ADVICE AND THEN SEE THE THING
      THROUGH.

THE ADVICE WAS TO BE TOUGHER AND TO ACT LIKE A
      BIG MAN,
AND I COULDN'T BE ACTING BIG LIKE THAT IF I RAN.
RUN I WOULD NOT, BUT I WAS NOT TO BE FURTHER
      MOLESTED,
IF IT WAS GOING TO BE BATTLE, THE COCK WOULD BE
      BESTED.

I NEEDED TOOLS THAT SHOWED THAT BIRD
 CONSIDERABLE POWER.
HIS LOT WOULD BE CROWING TO HENS; TO ME HE
 WOULD COWER!
 MY DAD WAS AN OLD FARMER, AND HE'D KNOW
 WHAT TO DO.
 I'D GET HIS ADVICE AND THEN SEE THE THING
 THROUGH.

DAD BECAME STRONGER IN HIS ADVICE TO A VERY
 YOUNG BOY,
"NEVER BRING DANGER TO LIVESTOCK, THEY ARE NOT
 TOYS!"
HE COULD SEE THAT I HAD A LITTLE MALICE IN MY
 BRAIN.
I THOUGHT WITH SOME FORCE THE BIRD COULD BE
 TRAINED.
SO I CONJURED A WHOLE PLAN, A STATEGIC WAY TO
 ATTACK.
I'D STAND MY GROUND FIRM, AND THEN GET SOME
 GROUND BACK.
 MY DAD WAS AN OLD FARMER, AND HE'D KNOW
 WHAT TO DO.
 I'D GET HIS ADVICE AND THEN SEE THE THING
 THROUGH.

"NO WAY," HE SAID WHEN HE HEAR HALF MY PLAN.
 "DON'T DARE.
YOU DO THAT TO THE BIRD, AND YOUR SCREAMS WILL
 SPLIT AIR."
BUT I WENT AHEAD, BECAUSE IT WAS MY BODY BEING
 HURT,
AND IT WAS BETWEEN ME AND A COCK AS WHO OWNED
 THE DIRT.
SO I OILED AN OLD LONG-REIN THAT WAS EXCESS TO
 STABLE
UNTIL IT, PLIANT AND LIMBER, WOULD BE WHIP AND
 CABLE.

MY DAD WAS AN OLD FARMER, AND HE'D KNOW
WHAT TO DO.
I'D GET HIS ADVICE AND THEN SEE THE THING
THROUGH.

"TOLD YOU'" HE SAID, "AND I MEANT IT, I'M HEARING
NO MORE.
YOU HANG UP THAT REIN, AND JUST GET TO DOING
YOUR CHORES."
WHEN THAT ROOSTER APPROACHED I WRAPPED HIS
NECK IN THE REIN
AND DRAGGED HIM TEN FEET, AND GOT READY TO DO
IT AGAIN.
I HAD WON! THAT COCK STAGGERED! I WAS FILLED
WITH SUCCESS!
PROBLEM WAS, THAT IN MY YOUTH I DIDN'T KNOW
WHAT COME NEXT
MY DAD WAS AN OLD FARMER, AND HE'D KNOW
WHAT TO DO.
I'D GET HIS ADVICE AND THEN SEE THE THING
THROUGH.

"DOGGONE," HE SAID, "YOU MAKE MORE PROBLEM
THAN I'LL CURE.
GET YOU OUT TO THE HOG HOUSE AND GET TO
CLEANING MANURE."
TIME HAD ELAPSED, I MIGHT MENTION IN TELLING; A
FEW WEEKS.
THAT ROOSTER WAS MORE OF A CHALLENGE AND HAD
NOT BECOME WEAK.
HE HAD DEVELOPED NECK MUSCLES THAT MATCHED A
BAD ATTITUDE,
AND MY CHORE TIME IN THE BARN YARD WAS AN
HECTIC INTERLUDE.
MY DAD WAS AN OLD FARMER, AND HE'D KNOW
WHAT TO DO.
I'D GET HIS ADVICE AND THEN SEE THE THING
THROUGH.

"THAT COCK," HE SAID, "JUST ALLOWS YOU TO MAKE
    A BIG STORY.
YOU GET CHORES DONE TIMELY, OR I'LL SEE THAT
    YOUR SORRY."
WITH THE REIN OILED AGAIN, AND AN ADDED SPLIT TO
    CRACK
AT THE END FOR SOME NOISE, I HAD WEAPON
    WITHOUT LACK.
I WAS GROWING BIGGER AND THE ROOSTER HAD
    GROWN MATURE,
BUT IT WAS STILL A BATTLE OF WHO GOT DRAGGED IN
    THE MANURE.
    MY DAD WAS AN OLD FARMER, AND HE'D KNOW
    WHAT TO DO.
    I'D GET HIS ADVICE AND THEN SEE THE THING
    THROUGH.

"I'LL SHOW YOU'" HE SAID, AS HE ROSE FROM
    OVERSTUFFED CHAIR,
"THAT THAT ROOSTER IS GENTLE, AND NOT CAUSE OF
    DESPAIR."
WE WERE WALKING TOGETHER WHEN THE COCK
    CLIMBED UP DAD'S LEG,
HOOKED IN HIS TALONS, BEAT WINGS, TOOK THE FIGHT
    UP A PEG.
DAD DROPPED STRAW HE HELD, SPILT SOME FEED,
    ACTED ANNOYED.
THEN HE REALIZED WHAT AN EXAMPLE SHOULD BE
    FOR HIS BOY.
    MY DAD WAS AN OLD FARMER, AND HE'D KNOW
    WHAT TO DO.

    I HEARD HIS FINAL ADVICE AS WE ATE CHICKEN
    STEW.

Hayfield Entomophobia

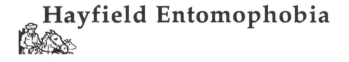

THIS YEAR WE HAVE SEEN NUMEROUS, VARIOUS
   GROUPS
OF THE LITTLE THINGS THAT CRAWL AND FLY IN LOOPS
BENEATH OUR CHINS AND ROUND OUR EARS.
WITH MANY LEGS AND WINGS THE GENERAL FORM,
THEY MAY BE SEEN ALONE, OR IN A SWARM
THAT SPLITS AND DOUBLY GROWS THROUGHOUT THE
   YEAR.

THE MORNING BRINGS THE MULTI-COLORED BUNCH
THAT BUZZ ROUND HEADS TILL TIME FOR LUNCH,
THEN CHANGES SHIFTS WITH SOME OF SOLID HUE
WHICH ARE KNOWN TO HUM AND STING AND CRAWL,
UNTIL ONE FEELS HE HAS ENDURED QUITE ALL
TO BE REQUIRED IN BLOODY DUES!

BUT YET, IT'S KNOWN THAT EVENING BRINGS
MINUTE BODIES ON TRANSPARENT WINGS
TO ASSURE ALL WAKING HOURS WRECKED.
SO WE KNOW THAT EACH SUMMER DAY
THOUGH ANTICIPATED PLEASANT, QUICKLY MAY
BE SPOILED BY SOME DANGED INSECT.

---

*A bedroll is poor protection from cold
if you're supposed to be on watch.*

 Part Two

Prairie

Prayers

Attendance

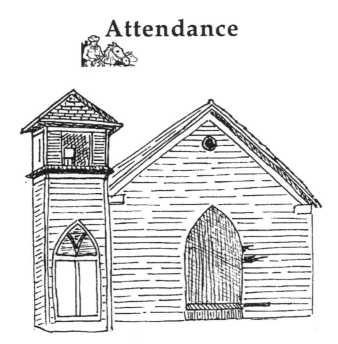

THE PREACHER SAYS I OUGHT TO BE IN CHURCH.
INSTEAD I WANT TO BE WHERE I WATCH SUN AND SKY.
HE SAYS THAT IN HIS BUILDING I SHOULD SEARCH
FOR PEACE OF MIND THAT EASY LETS ME DIE.

LORD, I DON'T WANT TO DIE. I JUST WANT TO
TAKE IT EASY HERE, AND BE AT PEACE WITH FOLKS.
THE PREACHER SAYS HE WANTS TO SEE ME THROUGH
THNGS TOUGH, BUT HE REALLY JUST PROVOKES.

HOW CAN HE HAVE ANSWERS ABOUT MY SIMPLE
    LIFE?
NEVER DOES HE RIDE THE MILES OUT TO MY PLACE.
AND WHY DOES HE ALWAYS SUGGEST I NEED A WIFE
TO TIDY UP, AND COOK, AND MAKE ME SHAVE MY
    FACE.

ONE, OR BOTH, OF US TWO CAN NOT TRULY
     UNDERSTAND.
HE QUOTES THINGS SAYING THE GRASS WILL ALWAYS
     GROW;
HE LOVES PEOPLE, BUILDINGS AND MONEY. I LOVE LAND,
AND COWS, AND FREEDOM TO ENJOY THE SPACE I KNOW.

I DON'T WANT HURT TO COME TO PLAGUE THE MAN.
SO I GOT UP A STORY TO KEEP HIS TEMPER DOWN.
IT KINDA EXPLAINS TO HIM RATHER SIMPLY HOW I AM,
THOUGH HE ACCEPTS IT WITH THE SLIGHTEST FROWN.

IT GOES LIKE THIS: "I'D GO TO CHURCH EXCEPT
THE WATER'S GOOD THIS YEAR. THE CREEK'S AFLOOD.
I'M THANKFUL TO HAVE WATER, BUT I'M NOT ADEPT
AT WASHING MY CLOTHES IN ROILING, FILTHY MUD.

"I WORK LIVESTOCK EVERY DAY, AND THEY'RE NOT
     CLEAN.
I'M NOT RICH, AND OWN ONLY ONE SET OF CLOTHES.
I HAVE TO BE NAKED WHEN THINGS DRY, WHICH SEEMS
AWHILE HUNG ON HITCHING RACK WHEN NO WIND BLOWS.

"AND WHEN THINGS ARE CLEANSED IN RISEN CREEKS
THE POCKETS FILL WITH SAND AND CRAWLING THINGS.
THOUGH NOT AFRAID OF GROWING SLIME OR THISTLE
     STICKS,
STICKY CLOTHES KEEP ME FROM FEELING LIKE A KING.

"I COULD COME IN WITHOUT A BATH OR LAUNDRY DONE.
WHO WOULD HEAR THE TALK WHILE SITTING THERE
     BESIDE?
NO ONE WOULD WORSHIP WELL, OR HAVE SOCIAL FUN,
AND THEY'D BE LATER INTO SAYING SOMETHING SNIDE.

"AND THEN THE PREACHER WOULD HAVE TO TALK
    WITH THEM,
SINCE THAT WOULD NEVER DO MID A CHRISTIAN CLAN!
BETTER SMELL TOO BAD OUT HERE AS ONE
    UNPOLISHED GEM
THAN COME ON IN AND FEEL THE HEAT OF
    "UNWASHED" BRAND."

LORD, YOU KNOW THERE IS A PROBLEM WITH ALL
    THIS!
WHAT AM I GOING TO SAY WHEN CREEKS GO CLEARLY
    DRY?
HE AIN'T BRIGHT, BUT KNOWS THAT SOMETHING IS
    AMISS.
HE IS STILL FOR NOW, BUT I KNOW AGAIN HE'LL TRY.

I AIN'T TOO BAD AT GETTING UP A TALE FOR ANYONE;
USUALLY STORIES COME QUICK AND EASY FROM MY
    LIPS.
BUT THAT IS WHEN WE'RE MERELY JOKING, HAVING
    FUN,
AND HOLDING NO MAN TO ACCOUNT FOR WHEN HE
    SLIPS.

NOW TELL ME, IS HE STRAIGHT AND I AM OUT OF
    LINE?
HAS MAN AND WEATHERED BUILDING GOT A CLAIM ON
    ME?
CAN'T I GIVE MY THANKS IN PRAYER AND PRIVATE TIME
RATHER THAN TO MOLD TO WHAT I NEVER WANT TO
    BE?

AMEN.

Why Me?

FATHER, HOW DO YOU KEEP IT ALL SORTED OUT?
YOU HELP WHATEVER I COME WITH, WHATEVER I BEG.
I DON'T SEE HOW ONE KNOWS WHAT ALL TO CONSIDER.
EVERY DAY SEEMS TO HAVE A NEW GROUP OF PLAGUES.

WHY IS HAVING MONEY SO IMPORTANT ?
WHY ARE OTHER PEOPLE JUST AS GREEDY AS I AM?

WHY DO LITTLE THINGS TAKE SO MUCH EFFORT?
WHY DO I SPEND EFFORT ON SO MANY LITTLE THINGS?

WHY CAN'T I BE ASSIGNED SOME INTERESTING WORK?
WHY CAN'T I ENJOY DOING THE WORK I'M ASSIGNED?

WHY AREN'T THERE MORE ADEQUATE EXPLANATIONS?
WHY CAN'T I UNDERSTAND EVERYTHING THAT'S
      EXPLAINED?

WHY DON'T THINGS ADD UP TO THE TOTALS OF LAST
    WEEK?
WHY AM I COMPLACENT WITH LAST WEEK'S VALUES?

WHY DO THE DESPICABLE PEOPLE HAVE SO MUCH
    INFLUENCE?
WHY DOES INFLUENCE MAKE ME SO DISPICABLE?

WHY CAN'T I BE HUMBLE WITHOUT BEING
    HUMILIATED?
WHY AM I EVER HUMILIATED ABOUT BEING HUMBLE?

YOUR FORMER SERVANTS HAVE BUILT BRIDGES;
WHEN THERE'S STREAMS TO CROSS, YOU HAVE
    PLANKS.
I DON'T EVEN KNOW WHERE THE LUMBER IS STACKED;
I'M LEFT TAKING HELP, OFFERING THANKS.

I TRULY DON'T MIND BEING THANKFUL.
BUT NEITHER DO I MIND HAVING LEARNED.
AND I WOULD LIKE TO HAVE ANSWERS
TO A FEW OF MY MAJOR CONCERNS!

AMEN.

Behind It All

WHAT A WONDERFUL WORLD YOU PUT TOGETHER.
IT IS A MARVEL TO WATCH THINGS UNFOLD.
LORD, HOW OFTEN DO YOU HAVE TO ADJUST
SOME LITTLE THING THAT'S RUSTED AND OLD?

I'M AMAZED AT NATURE FITTING TOGETHER
WITH NO BOLT OR SCREW OR SMOOTH WIRE.
AND HOW THINGS ARE ALWAYS IN THEIR PLACE
LIKE MAYBE YOU WAS EXPECTING A BUYER.

I BEEN THINKING ABOUT THAT OLD COW'S TAIL
THAT SHE USES TO CHASE OFF THE FLIES,
THAT WHACKS THE CARELESS YOUNG MILKER,
AND GETS LIFTED FROM THE WAY OF COW PIES.

THAT TAIL IS AN ENGINEER'S GLORY
WITH JOINTS AND COVERING AND SWITCH
THAT TOGETHER WORK WITH SMALL EFFORT,
AND CONNECT TO A SMALL SPINAL NICHE.

WITH FLAILING TAIL, THE COW SHOWS DISLEASURE
BUT WHEN PEACEFUL JUST LETS IT FALL.
IT NEVER IS FIXED WHERE HEAD OUGHT TO BE;
LENGHTH IS ADJUSTED TO COW, SHORT OR TALL.

CAN I LEARN TO PUT THINGS IN SUCH ORDER?
WILL YOU HELP ME TO FIND WHAT TO DO
TO HAVE MY JUMBLED LIFE STRAIGHTENED OUT?
I DON'T DO WELL BY MYSELF; I NEED YOU.

AMEN

Chinook

LORD, CAN WE HAVE A WARM WIND FOR A COUPLE DAYS?
WE HAVE LITTLE TROUBLE WITH FOG OR EVENING HAZE.
THE COLD'S NOT BAD 'CAUSE WE KNOW HOW TO BUNDLE
    UP,
AND QUEEN'S TAUGHT THE SKILL OF WARMTH TO HER PUP.
SITTING NEAR THE FIRE MAKES A PLEASANT TIME AT DARK
WHEN DRIFTED SNOW HAS LEFT THE LAND WITHOUT A
    MARK.
EACH MORNIMG WE BREAK NEW ROAD TO FEED HUNGRY
    STOCK
AS BEAMS BREAK FROM WHERE THE SUN'S BEEN LOCKED.
BACK HERE BETWEEN TWO LOW RIDGES LIFE'S JUST FINE
AS WE REPAIR AND PUTTER THROUGH A QUIET TIME.
BUT A WARM WIND WOULD BE TERRIBLE WELCOME ANY
    DAY.
AT ANY HOUR, A CHINOOK COULD WELL BE SENT OUR WAY!
THE THING IS THAT WE HAVE A FESTERING CONCERN
ABOUT A THING THAT BUNK HOUSE BOYS SELDOM LEARN.
WE WON'T DRAW PAY OR LEAVE, WE'LL TAKE THE LOAD,
IF YOU'LL MELT THE SNOW ENOUGH TO OPEN UP THE ROAD.
YOU SEE, THE BOSS HAS PROMISED, AND IT'S TIME TO DO
SOMETHING STRONG ABOUT THIS CAUSE FOR CRY AND
    HUE.
ONE TRIP TO TOWN GETS A YOUNG BOSS OFF THE HOOK;
HE TAKES ONE MAN IN, AND BRINGS OUT A BETTER COOK!

AMEN.

Anger

LORD, IT WAS FUNNY, REALLY, HOW SHE STOMPED!
BUT IT WASN'T FAIR THAT WE ALL LAUGHED.
SHE WAS SO CONCERNED ABOUT SUCH SILLINESS,
AND MADE SUCH AN FUSS ABOUT THAT CALF.

NOW, WE WAS JUST ROPING THAT LITTLE CRITTER
FOR SOME PRACTICE, NOT ONE TIGHT LOOP!
WE SHOOK 'EM OFF AS FAST AS THEY WENT ON
AND JOKED WHO WAS "BEST ROPER IN THE GROUP".

THE CALF WAS "ALFIE", THE LITTLE ORPHAN
WE BOTTLED WHEN HIS MA DIED IN DEEP SNOW.
HE SLEEPS IN THE BUNKHOUSE 'CAUSE THE BOYS
ARE TOO SOFT TO TURN HIM OUT, YOU KNOW.

ALFIE" HAS FELT SO MANY HANDS UPON HIS HEAD
THAT HE NEVER FELT THE DROPPING OF THE ROPE.
IT WAS DONE AT WALKING PACE; WE WOULD HAVE
DROPPED THE MAN THAT CAME AT ALFIE ON A LOPE.

SO, WE WERE SURE SURPRISED WHEN THAT CITY GAL
STOOD THERE AND USED LANGUAGE MEANT FOR US.
I MEAN, THE WORDS WE USE WHEN WE'RE NOT RIGHT,
EVERYTHING IN THE GROUP CALLED SWEAR AND CUSS.

AND WE DIDN'T ANSWER 'CAUSE WE WERE SO
        SURPRISED
THAT SHE DIDN'T KNOW HOW CAREFUL WE HAD BEEN.
AND WE ACCEPTED ALL THE THINGS SHE SAID 'BOUT
        US
ROUGH AND WORTHLESS MEN WHO SEEM SO BENT ON
        SIN.

STILL, WE NEED TO BE FORGIVEN FOR THAT LAUGHTER
THAT WILL STICK TIGHT AS LONG AS SHE'S ALIVE.
UNTIL SHE STOMPED HER FOOT, SHE DIDN'T KNOW SHE
STOOD IN A COW PIE FROM YESTERDAY'S DRIVE.

HEAVEN HELP US!, AMEN.

The Gal in Town

FATHER, HOW IS IT I ALWAYS NEED SO MUCH HELP?
WHY AREN'T THINGS SET IN MY MIND LIKE OTHER FOLK?
SURELY, EVERYONE HAS TROUBLE THINKING THROUGH
SOME THINGS THAT I'M ALWAYS BRINGING UP TO YOU.

NOW, I'LL BE HEADED TO TOWN IN JUST A COUPLE DAYS
FOR GOODS, AND TO SEE HOW WELL THE MARKET PAYS.
AND IT'S A DAY'S RIDE AT A STRONG HORSES' PACE,
SO I HAVE TO BE OVER NIGHT AND STAY SOME PLACE.

THE LAND IS ALL BOUGHT UP SOME MILES FROM TOWN,
AND SQUATTERS DON'T WANT TO SEE ME BEDDED DOWN
ON THEIR GROUND. EVEN THOUGH THEY AIN'T PAID
FOR IT YET; IT'S FENCED AND A CLAIMS BEEN LAID.

But THEY AREN'T MY TROUBLE. IT'S THE PRETTY GIRL
WHO WORKS THE SALOON, WHO GIVES THE MEN A WHIRL.
I CAN'T ARRANGE A ROOM WITHOUT HER COMING ROUND
STRIKING UP SOME TALK, OR ASKING WHERE I'M BOUND.

I KNOW HOW SHE WORKS TO KEEP THE WOLF FROM DOOR,
AND I HAVEN'T USED HER SERVICES ANY TIME BEFORE.
I'M NOT FEELING LIKE DOING ANY WRONG THING NOW
BUT I FEEL I SHOULD MAKE THINGS BETTER SOMEHOW.

I'VE NO REASON TO BE RUDE OR CHASE THE GAL AWAY
BUT AFTER TALKING WITH HER, WHAT DO OTHERS SAY?
NEITHER OF US NEED SUFFER UNKIND WORDS FROM JERKS
WHO MAKE GUILTY, TRASHY TALK WITH THE HOTEL CLERK.

And I'M NO TRAIL HAND RIDING IN AND OUT SO FREE
OF SINGLE THOUGHT OF HOW THE WORLD SHOULD BE.
SO I CAN SEE THAT GAL COULD BE CUTE INSIDE;
SOMETHINGS WRONG THAT MAKES HER REAL SELF HIDE.

THOSE AROUND HER NEVER SEEM TO THINK OR CARE
ABOUT HER LIFE BEYOND THEIR USE, OR CURLY HAIR.
I WONDER HOW SHE GOT TO BE LIVING SUCH A LIFE;
WAS IT CARELESSNESS THAT STARTED ALL HER STRIFE?

THE PEOPLE IN THAT TOWN USE HER TO BE AMUSED.
THEY'RE NOT CAREFUL HOW HER REPUTATION'S USED,
BUT TAKE HER DOLLARS SENT TO CHURCH OR GUILD
FOR FIRE OR FLOOD RELIEF OR SIMPLY COFFER FILLED.

IT'S OKAY THAT SHE PROTECTS THE YOUNG FROM BULLY
OR TENDS TO THE MAN SHOT IN THE STREET IN FOLLY,
OR MENDS CLOTHES AND SPIRITS OF TATTERED PEOPLE,
SO LONG AS THEY DON'T HAVE TO BE FIXING THE FEEBLE.

HER DAYS DON'T EVER GET FILLED WITH FUN OR PRANK
SHE RARELY HEARS THE SOUND OF WORDS OF THANKS.
AND I'M NO HELP IN BRINGING A SMILE HER WAY
WHEN I FEEL THE PRESSURE OF WHAT OTHER PEOPLE SAY.

I'D LIKE TO TAKE HER HOME AND SET HER TO THE CHORES!
SHE NEEDS SOME TIME TO SLOWLY RELAX IN OUT-OF-
   DOORS.
SHE COULD TEND THE GARDEN AND THE GUERNSEY COW.
NOT ONCE, I BET WOULD I EVEN HAVE TO SHOW HER HOW.

BUT I'D HAVE THE PLAGUE OF MEN WHO'D PROWL THE
   PLACE
INTENT ON MAKING MISERY AND LAYING PEOPLE WASTE.
TOWN FIGHTS AND FEUDS WOULD BE ON MY LAND INSTEAD,
AND IN A RUCKUS SOMEONE WOULD BE RILED, AND DEAD.

SEE, ALL I WANT TO DO IS GO TO TOWN AND SELL MY
   COWS,
BUT IT ISN'T QUIET BUSINESS THAT THE PLACE ALLOWS.
FATHER, AS I SAID, I NEED HELP TO GET IT SORTED OUT
SO I TREAT HER RIGHT, AND PUT THE OTHER STUFF TO
   ROUT.

HELP ME CALM MY MIND!   AMEN.

*The kids learn poor music if you sing
a different hymn at home than you
sing at church.*

Prayer of Town

LORD, KEEP ME OUT OF ANY TOWN;
DON'T LET A SOFT LIFE WEIGH ME DOWN.
DON'T LET ME BECOME LIKE THOSE
FELLERS SITTING 'ROUND IN FANCY CLOTHES.
I NEED TO FEEL THE EARLY BREEZES
THAT WAKE A MAN AS HIS HORSE EASES
OVER A RISE AND SNUFFS AT CATTLE
THAT MAKE THE AUTUMN WILLOW RATTLE.
IN LIFE WE EACH WILL HAVE OUR PLACE,
BUT MINE DON'T NEED TO BE NEAR LACE.
GINGHAM IS GOOD ENOUGH FOR EVERY DAY
AND LET OILCLOTH ON MY TABLE STAY.
KEEP ME OUT OF TOWN, AWAY FROM STRIFE.
PLEASE, LET ME HAVE A SIMPLE LIFE.
I WANT TO BE FREE UPON SOME LAND
WHETHER ITS ROCKS OR WIND BLOWN SAND.
WHERE THERE'S GRASS I NEED NO COIN
OR PAPER SCRIP TO PAY FOR GOIN'.
KEEP ME FREE TO RIDE TO WHAT I'LL SEE,
AND I'LL SING PRAISES UNTO THEE!

AMEN.

Homestead Dedication

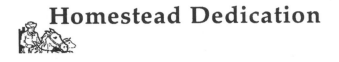

LORD, I PAID THE CASH AND GOT A CLAIM
SO I COULD TRY A PIECE OF GROUND TO TAME.
I AIN'T BEEN THIS FAR WEST BEFORE
AND I ADMIT I'M SCARED TO THE CORE!

I'M ONE OF THEM YOU HAVE ALWAYS BLESSED
NOW I NEED HELP TO GET THROUGH THIS TEST.
BUT I'VE DECIDED THAT IT'S JUST FINE
IF YOU GET ALL OF THE PAYOFF THIS TIME.

SO HERE IS HOW I INTEND TO RUN THE PLACE:
I'LL WORK ALL DAY, AT MEALS SAY GRACE,
READ FROM YOUR BOOK, TO MY WIFE STAY WED.
I'LL FEED THE STRANGER, IF NEED, OFFER BED.

I'LL BE CAREFUL TO DO SPENDING THAT'S WISE,
I WON'T GIVE UP TILL I GIVE 'ER THREE TRIES.
I'LL NOT SWEAR AT MULES, NOR WHIP A HORSE,
I'LL MILK ON TIME, AND SAVE WATER, OF COURSE.

I'LL STAY AT HOME LEST THERE'S A POSITIVE NEED
TO BE SOMEWHERE ELSE, AND DOIN' YOUR DEEDS.
WHAT FORTUNE YOU SEND ME WILL BE QUICK
        ACCEPTED;
I'LL LISTEN IN PRAYERS TO SEE WHAT EXPECTED.

I'LL GIVE YOU PRAISES EVEN WHEN WATER IS SHORT.
TO SAVE ON DOCTORIN', I'LL QUIT PICKIN' MY WART.
I'M GOING TO BE HUMBLE AS THE PRODIGAL BOY
AND GIVE YOU THE CREDIT WITHOUT BEIN' COY.

Now, I AIN'T SO DULL AS TO THINK THIS BE EDEN,
SO UP FRONT I'M TELLING WHAT I'LL LIKELY BE
	NEEDIN'.
THIS PLACE NEEDS BLESSED! THE GROUND'S JUST
	FAIR
AND IT'LL NEED ALL THE HELP AN ANGEL CAN SPARE.

I'LL NEED MOISTURE ON GROUND, BUT NONE ON MY
	SADDLE.
IF SEED COMES ON TIME, MY BRAIN WON'T GET
	ADDLED.
MY SODDY HOUSE CAN SURE DO WITHOUT TICKS OR
	FLEAS,
AND I'D LIKE DO WITHOUT CHILLS, OR FEVER OR
	SNEEZE.

AND THE LIVESTOCK NEEDS A WARM WINTER THIS
	YEAR;
CAN COYOTES DRIFT WHERE WE CAN CALVE WITHOUT
	FEAR?
HARNESS AND TOOLS NEED YOUR STRENGTH TO MOVE
	SOIL
'CAUSE WE WON'T MAKE HEADWAY JUST USING UP
	TOIL.

I KNOW, THOUSANDS OF YEARS YOU HAVE TENDED
	THE PLACE,
BUT I'M ASKING SPECIAL BLESSINGS JUST FOR THIS
	CASE.
ALONG WITH SOME GOOD WATER IN BOTH SKY AND
	CRICK,
I'LL WATCH OUT FOR WARM SUN TO MAKE THE HAY
	THICK.

BY GOLLY, I'LL NEED SOME HELP ABOUT THINGS I
    DON'T KNOW.
I'M FROM SOUTH CAROLINA, CAN YOU TELL ME ABOUT
    SNOW?
I PLAN TO ERECT A TRIPOD WITH A TEN-BLADED WIND
    MILL;
WHERE COMES DRINKING WATER IF THINGS SUDDENLY
    GO STILL?

THERE IS JUST BARELY GROUND TO HANDLE ONE
    MAN'S NEEDS.
PLEASE CLEAR THE BUFFALO SO THEY DON'T TRAMPLE
    SEEDS.
THE MAIL! I'LL NEED MAIL TO KEEP INFORMED OF THE
    EARTH,
NEW METHODS OF FARMING, AND WHEN SISTER GIVES
    BIRTH.

BUT THIS PRAYER AIN'T OFFERED JUST TO CRAVE
    THINGS,
IT OUGHT TO BE CLEAR THAT I'LL OFFERINGS BRING.
IT IS YOURS, AND I WANT TO RUN IT YOUR WAY.
IF I CAN'T PROVE THE CLAIM, THEN YOU CAN TAKE IT
    AWAY.

AMEN.

Swallows

FATHER, HAVE YOU BEEN WATCHING THOSE BIRDS
BY THE BRIDGE, FLYING WITH THEIR MOUTHS OPEN?
HOW CAN THEY LIVE ON INSECTS SO EASY?
HOW DO THEY FIND THEM BUT HOPING AND GROPING?

IT REALLY IS THE QUICK AND THE DEAD WITH THEM.
THE BUG OR THE BIRD MUST REALLY BE FAST!
THOSE BIRDS TURN CORNERS FASTER THAN MY
CUTTING HORSE, FOR A MIGHTY GRIMY REPAST.

I THINK MY LIFE IS LIKE THOSE INSECT-EATERS.
I LIVE IN A MUD HUT JUST OFF THE CREEK.
I TAKE WHAT THE LAND OFFERS FOR COMFORTS,
AND A FULL BELLY PUTS LIFE AT A PEAK.

BUT I DON'T GET TO DRIFT SOUTH IN LATE FALL.
I STAY HERE BUCKING DRIFTS, FEEDING HAY.
MY LITTLE ONES DON'T LEAVE THE NEST IN FLIGHT,
SO I NEED YOU EASING MY LIFE EVERY DAY.

AMEN.

---

*A prayer gets heard better if the
knee and the heart bend together.*

Stories

OH LORD! WE REALLY ARE GLAD THAT WE HAVE
    LIES.
IT'S THE THING THAT TIES THE WORKIN' MEN
    TOGETHER.
IN THE LONG COLD NIGHTS, WHAT WOULD WE DO IF
    WE
COULDN'T STORY OUT THE TIME 'BOUT HAIR AND
    FEATHER.

NOW, WE DON'T WANT TO DARKEN UP THE PLACE
    WITH FEAR
OR FILTH, OR THINGS THAT HURT THE FOLKS AROUND.
BUT, WE *CAN* LIVEN UP A LIFE OR TWO WITH
    DESCRIPTION
OF WHAT <u>COULD MAYBE</u> HAVE HAPPENED ON THIS
    GROUND.

SURE, THERE IS ON EVERY PLACE THE CHANCE THAT
    SOME
ORDINARY PEOPLE DID GOOD THINGS AS YET UNTOLD.
AND WHAT A WASTE, IF WE COULDN'T FIND A WAY TO
    SHOW
HOW EXTRA HEARTILY THEY WORKED, OR BOUGHT AND
    SOLD.

GRANTED, THE BIRDS MAY NOT HAVE FLOWN QUITE
    SO HIGH
OR FAR AS MEN CAN SEE THEM ACROSS THE BUNK
    HOUSE.
AND HORSES MAY BUCK JUST A TAD ABOVE THE
    RAFTER
IN TELLIN' OF YOUNG STOCK MEETIN' UP WITH
    GROUSE.

No picture on canvas, or from camera, offers
    much.
Thy nature can't be measured with the artist
    brush.
But mental work can conjure up a scene so
    complete
In fine detail, that the memory can't be
    crushed.

We haven't much; we get strong about what
    there is,
Or how bad we lack, or what got away in other
    days.
The dealings with other folks maybe could
    have been
A little easier than how we explain things away.

Now, when our mistakes cause misery to a
    soul and

PROVOKES SOME FEELINGS THAT AREN'T WHAT YOU
    WANT,
SOMEONE WILL TURN IT ROUND AGAIN AND TELL
    THINGS
SO STRAIGHT THAT WE'LL GET APOLOGY FOR TAUNT.

So LORD, LET US HAVE LIES TO TELL EACH OTHER,
ABOUT WHERE WE GO, AND WHAT WE SEE, AND WHAT
    WE DO.
WE'LL PROMISE TO KEEP 'EM HARMLESS OF ANY ONE,
AND WE'LL KEEP STRAIGHT ALONG THE LINE WITH YOU.

AMEN.

While Riding

LORD, IT IS HOT ON THE GRASSLAND
AND THERE ISN'T SHADE FOR MILES.
READING SCRIPTURE OUT HERE TAKES EFFORT
AND *ALL* THE FAITH OF A CHILD.

HOW ABOUT THEM "RIVERS OF WATER"?
I HAVE ONLY SINKHOLES I'VE CUSSED.
AND "EVERY MAN AND HIS FIG TREE"
DOESN'T MAKE SENSE IN THIS DUST.

I DON'T GET TOSSED WITH THE WAVES
OUT HERE, EXCEPT HEAT WAVES IN JULY.
AND THE ONLY WATER WE'VE KNOWN THIS
YEAR IS STILL A STREAK IN THE SKY.

SOMEHOW THE GRASS KEEPS SEEDING BACK
AND SUPPORTS A FEW LONELY COWS.
AND I'VE AGREED TO RIDE THE MILES
AND AT NIGHT TO HEAR COYOTES HOWL.

DO YOU HEAR THOSE DOGS BEFORE ME?
IS NATURE IN SOME ORDERD WAY?
WHAT IS THE RANK OF A COWHAND
COMPARED TO A MAN FARMING HAY?

I READ YOUR GOOD BOOK TO LEARN THINGS
BUT OFTEN I DON'T UNDERSTAND.
I WISH YOU'D CONSIDER AUTOMATICALLY
BLESSING ANYONE WHO WORKS ON THE LAND!

AMEN.

Steps

FATHER,

THESE OLD STEPS ARE BUILT JUST RIGHT
TO SIT AND WHITTLE INTO NIGHT.
THEN BOOTS ARE COVERED BY SLIVERS
FROM WILLOWS FOUND 'LONG THE RIVER.

THERE IS SOMETHING ABOUT A KNIFE
THAT CUTS AWAY ONE'S STRIFE.
AS IT EASES THE BARK FROM A BRANCH
A MAN CONSIDERS THE NEEDS OF HIS RANCH.

WHEN THE MOON RISES OVER CORRAL POST
AND THE AIR TAKES ON SOME FROST,
I KNOW I'VE PONDERED LONG ENOUGH
FOR ONE EVENING ON ONE DAY'S STUFF.

THEN I'M GRATEFUL FOR A PLACE AND TIME
TO FORGET A RANCH'S DUST AND GRIME.
AND I FEEL OBLIGED FOR STEPS LIKE THESE
THAT HELP ME PONDER ABOUT THANKS TO THEE.

AMEN.

The Request

Lord, I've come to ask for several things.
My life seems to be a big request.
I'm willing to beg for everything or
anything to stop satan in the west.

And now that I've gotten started
and you know how it is that I feel;
I just realized how much I have,
and that only in thanks should I kneel.

Forgive me!

Amen.

A Heathen Prayer

FATHER, I HEARD A DISTURBING PIECE
OF TALK FROM A HEATHEN TONGUE.
AN INDIAN MAN WRAPPED UP IN BUCKSKIN
AND DECKED OUT WITH FEATHERS RAISED
HIS HANDS, NOT KNOWING I WAS NEAR.

HE SAID THANKS FOR EVERYTHING,
ALL HE HAD, OR HOPED TO GET. ALL
HE'D LOST, AND WHAT HAD BEEN TAKEN
FROM HIM. HE WAS TALKING TO HIS GOD,
AND I BEGAN TO WONDER IF THAT'S YOU.

HE SPOKE SO SOFT OF LOVE OF WIFE AND
CHILD THAT I FORGOT HIM TO BE SAVAGE.
THAT UNTAMED RED MAN HAD SUCH HOPES
OF DOING RIGHT AND HONEST THAT I
COULD NOT CONCEAL MY SHAME.

HE WISHED HIS FRIENDS, AND FELLOW BRAVE
OF BATTLE, WOULD LIVE FOREVER BLESSED.
AND THAT THE TRIBES HE FOUGHT WOULD BE
TOO STRONG FOR HIM TO SPEAK OF
WEAK WARRIORS' ROUND HIS FIRES.

BUT WHAT REALLY GOT ME STIRRED WAS
WHEN HE ASKED ETERNAL HELP FOR ME!
HE'LL STEAL AND FIGHT TO MAKE ME GO
AWAY, BUT ASKS HIS GOD TO HELP HIM
DO IT SOMEHOW RIGHT AND GOOD.

HE WORRIES THAT I DON'T KNOW THE
LAND ENOUGH TO MAKE A WINTER.
HE KNOWS MY COW CAN'T BE LEFT TO
DRIFT, AND I WON'T EAT MY DOG.
I'M HIS "WEAK WHITE BROTHER."

DID NATURE GIVE HIM SUCH A SOUL AT BIRTH
FOR HIM TO WORRY OVER ALL THE EARTH?
I GET CONCERNED ABOUT A QUARTER
SECTION OF GRASS WHILE HE EMBRACES
ALL I'VE NEVER LEARNED TO KNOW.

HE MADE ME WONDER WHAT HEATHEN REALLY
IS, AND WHO QUALIFIES TO BE YOUR CHILD,
AND WHAT YOU WANT FROM US. WHILE
I'M HUMBLE, PLEASE TEACH ME ENOUGH
TO BE EQUAL TO A HEATHEN!

AMEN.

Preacher and Friends

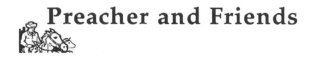

FATHER, I DO LOVE YOUR SPIRIT
AND LIKE HAVING IT FOLLOW AROUND.
BUT I NEVER CAN QUITE UNDERSTAND
WHY SOME OF THE DUMB PEOPLE ABOUND.

NOW, TAKE THE CASE OF THE PREACHER
AND THE FOLKS HE SENDS TO THIS PLACE.
THE STUPID THINGS THEY SAY AND DO!
THEIR THINKING IS WAY OFF ITS BASE.

I WANT THIS PLACE AS YOU MADE IT
WITH WILD GRASS AND FLOWERS AND BIRDS.
THE THINKING OUT HERE IS CLEAN AS THE WIND
AND THE BEAUTY OUT-DOES PRETTY WORDS.

THIS RANCH IS NO PLACE TO BE DIRTY,
DROPPING THEIR TRASH ON THE GROUND,
LEAVING THE PLACE CLUTTERED AND FILTHY
LIKE THE WAY THEY LIVE IN THEIR TOWN.

THEY COME ALONG, TALKING REPENTANCE
WHEN I HAVE DONE NOTHING WRONG.
THEY JUDGE ME FOR BEING LIKE OTHERS
AND WANT ME SINGING ONLY THEIR SONG.

I DO MY OWN THINKING AND WORKING.
I DON'T HAVE TO HIRE THE TOWN DRUNK
TO FEEL GOOD UNDER A PAMPERED HIDE
AT NIGHT, AS I FALL ASLEEP ON MY BUNK.

HEY! WHAT GOES AT THEIR HOMESTEAD
THAT THEY HAVE TIME TO FRET ME?
ISN'T THERE STOCK OR A GROWING CROP
OVER WHICH THEY NEED TO SEE?

NOW, THE PREACHER SAYS YOU HIRED HIM,
BUT THAT I'M TO BE PAYING HIS BILLS.
I'M NOT SO SURE IF THAT IS THE CASE
AND I AIN'T AFFORDING NO FRILLS!

I PUT UP WITH THEIR UNTIMELY VISITS.
I LET THEM TRASH AND TALK ALL THEY WANT.
BUT IN MY SOUL I DON'T GIVE 'EM CREDIT,
'CAUSE I KNOW THAT YOU PRIME MY FOUNT.

AMEN.

*You don't need to write a contract if
you are both really Christian.*

Part Three

Gibberish

and

Generalities

The Winner

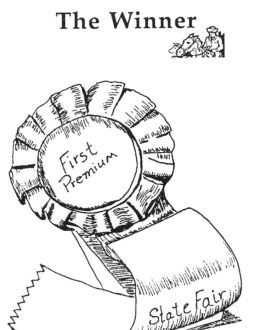

I DON'T NEED TO PLACE AS FIRST.
I DON'T NEED TO BE TOP DOG.
I DON'T NEED THE ACCOLADES
OR TO DRIFT IN DREAMLAND FOG.

I DON'T EVEN NEED TO RANK.
I DON'T COVET SECOND PLACE.
I DON'T CARE ABOUT AWARDS
AND LOSING ISN'T LOSING FACE.

I DON'T WANT YOUR FAME, MY FRIEND.
I DON'T NEED BE SEEN AS FUNNY.
I DON'T NEED REAL FAMOUS POEMS.
PLEASE, JUST BUY MY STUFF FOR MONEY.

Bear

THE OLD MAN STEPPED TO THE FIRELIGHT
AND BREATHED IN THE COOL MOUNTAIN AIR.
HE LOOKED TO THE HEAVENS, AND STARLIGHT,
AND STARTED TO TALK ABOUT ... **BEAR**.

HE LIVED MANY LONG YEARS ON THE HILLSIDE,
AND HAD SEEN SCAT AND PAW PRINT GALORE.
HE HAD MET AN OLD SOW WITH CUBS ALONG SIDE,
AND FELT SOLID FEAR TO HIS CORE.

HE HAD SEEN GRIZZLY FEED IN THE MEADOW
ON LUSH GRASSES, AND BERRIES, AND SUCH
AS MAKES THEM FAT BEFORE WINTER SNOW;
A PICTURE TO SEE, BUT NOT TOUCH.

HE RESPECTED THE STRENGTH AND THE GRACE
OF THOSE CANINES OF EXCELLENT SIZE.
HE'D JUDGE THEIR MASS FROM THE LENGTH OF PACE
AND GAVE THEM RANGE THAT WAS WIDE.

STILL, HIS HOUNDS WERE OFTEN OUT TRAILING
SOME ORNERY BEAR THAT LIKED SHEEP,
AND THEY NEVER WERE KNOWN FOR THEIR FAILING
TO PUT A BEAR FOREVER ASLEEP.

HE UNDERSTOOD THE USES OF BEAR PARTS.
AT NIGHT HIS BLANKET WAS HIDES,
HIS STEW INCLUDED BLACK BEAR HEARTS
AND WAS A MEAL DESERVING HIS PRIDE.

Brown BEAR GAVE UP THEIR LARGE TENDONS
FOR HIS USE AS TETHERING STRINGS.
AND BEAR STEAKS SLOWLY FRIED BY THE POND
BECAME A GASTRONOMICAL THING.

He TREKKED FAR TO NORTHWARD FOR POLARS
AND BROUGHT BACK A PRETTY WHITE HIDE.
NEVER HAD A HUNT BEEN MUCH COLDER,
BUT THE MEAT MADE HIM WARMER INSIDE.

The OLD MAN HAS ADVICE FOR YOUNG FOLK,
WHICH HE WANTS THEM EVER TO HEED.
NEVER HUNT BEAR WITH A MAN WHO WILL JOKE,
AND HUNT NOT AT ALL, WITHOUT NEED.

When YOU FALL, AND PAIN IS A FLIRTIN',
RUB BEAR GREASE ON BRUISES THAT HURT.
BEAR MEDICINE IS HEALING FOR CERTAIN.
AND LAST, EAT CINNAMON BEAR FOR DESSERT.

If you are good all the time,
you are getting better.

The Crossroads Poems

Many poems tell of the fork in the road,
or crossroads where choices are made.
They tell long stories of consequence,
and to morally live we are bade.

The tales of those who wrongfully chose
include lives twisted and torn;
and the folks who left another behind
end up sad and forgotten, forlorn.

Somehow the folk who see through the haze
and determine what road is the best,
are rewarded with gifts befitting the wise
and honored for passing the test.

Choices are given as the good and the bad;
there is never a way to return.
Choices made at a cross in the road
determine what lessons we learn.

As we improve more roads will appear
that bring us service and peace.
And if we degrade, some road will lead
to poor torment never to cease.

Poets haven't seen my dilemma in life;
I miss the theory/reality joint.
For I never get a crossroads in sight,
I'm always at a 'five points'.

The Weather Report

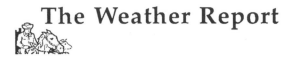

I AIN'T GONNA TALK ABOUT WEATHER.
I WON'T TELL OF THE HORRORS I'VE SEEN.
I WON'T BE COAXED TO IT, NEITHER,
I WON'T TELL WHAT HEAVEN'S SIGNS MEAN.

I WON'T TELL OF THE STORMS I LIVED THROUGH
OR HOW THE ELEMENTS WORKED ON MY LIFE.
OR HOW I WAS BEAT, THOUGH I STOOD ON MY FEET
AND REFUSED TO BOW TO THE STRIFE.

I WON'T SAY HOW DEEP SNOW FALLS,
OR HOW THE BREEZE PILES IT UP.
OR HOW THE FENCE DISAPPEARED,
OR THE FATE OF THE LONG-LEGGED PUP.

I WON'T RELATE THE COLD AND THE WET
OF QUICK CHANGES IN SPRING OR THE FALL.
I WON'T RECALL THE HOT AND THE SWEAT
DRIPPING FROM MEN SHORT AND TALL.

I WON'T REMARK TOWARD THE SUNSET
AND THE DUST STORM THAT CAUSED IT TO SHOW,
NOR ALL THE EVENTS WHEN WE LOST ALL THE HAY
FROM THE FIRE SET BY NOTHING WE KNOW.

I WON'T THINK AGAIN OF A RAINY CORRAL,
I NEVER TALK OF DEEP SLIMY MUD ANYMORE,
AND I ACKNOWLEDGE NO FILTH IN THE HOUSE
"LESS IT'S <u>MY</u> BOOTS THAT DIRTY THE FLOOR.

I WON'T TATTLE ABOUT THE BIG CULVERT
THAT GOT PLUGGED BY A FLOOD IN A FLASH.
AND I AIN'T GONNA PRATTLE OR MAKE NOISE
ABOUT THE TOILETS THAT STOPPED UP WITH TRASH.

I WON'T CHAT CONCERNING FIELDS BARREN DRY
WITH PUFFS UNDER FOOT WHILE I WALKED,
AND THIN COWS DRIFTING SO SLOWLY ALONG
THAT TOURISTS TOOK PICTURES AND GAWKED.

I WON'T EXPLAIN HOW AIR HUNG ONTO WATER
AND MADE MY CLOTHES WRINGING WET,
OR TURNED IT ALL LOOSE TO GO BACK TO SEA,
AND DEHYDRATED MY SOUL AS I SAT.

I WON'T UTTER A WORD ABOUT FOG,
THE SOUP THAT I'VE TRAVELED THROUGH.
STORIES OF DOING ALL THINGS WITHOUT SEEING
WOULD MOST SURELY BE BORING TO YOU.

I WON'T BLATHER ABOUT CLOUDS IN THE AIR
WITH DARKNESS AND NOISE, CRASHES AND BOOMS,
DESTRUCTION AND TUMULT, CHAOS AND DIN,
HAVOC UNHEARD OF, AND RUIN AND DOOM.

I WON'T START GOSSIP ABOUT THE HIGH WIND
'CAUSE IT COULDN'T BE SEEN. WHAT IT CARRIED
WAS HALF THE FIELDS FROM OUR COUNTY TO
WHEREVER IT WENT, WHERE SOMEONE GOT BURIED.

I WON'T SPOUT OFF ABOUT HOW I COULDN'T SEE
WITH THE CEILING SO LOW THAT DUCKS WOULDN'T FLY
WHEN THE VISIBILITY DROPPED TO DOWN ABOUT THREE,
AND MY PILOT FRIEND SAW THE TORNADO'S EYE.

I WON'T GO ON (THOUGH I'M TEMPTED) ABOUT ICE,
AND FLAILING CARTWHEELS PERFORMED IN THE FIELD.
I COULDN'T BEGIN TO RELATE ALL THE NICE
THINGS THAT NEIGHBORS DID WHILE I HEALED.

ALL MY WEATHER STORIES ARE LOST OR DON'T COUNT.
THERE IS A DOUBTER WHENEVER I SPEAK.
NOW, PROOF OF THE WEATHER CAN ALWAYS BE SEEN
AND EXPLAINED BY THE MAP ON THE TEEVEE SCREEN.

About God

HAVE YOU EVER WONDERED ABOUT GOD,
WHAT HE PUT TOGETHER IN A WEEK,
HOW HE GOT US ALL IN PROPER PAIRS,
AND MADE SO MANY THINGS UNIQUE?
THE MASSIVE MAJESTY OF MOUNTAINS,
THE WILD GRASSES OF FLATTENED PLAINS,
THE ETERNAL MOTION OF FLOWING RIVERS,
AND LAND THAT'S ONLY WASHED BY RAIN.
THE MUSIC OF HIS NATURAL WORLD
SOOTHES OR WARNS IN UNITY TO NEED,
FROM BREEZE TO WARNING CALL OF BIRD
THAT CREATION'S OTHER CRITTERS HEED.
THEN THERE'S WHAT HE DID WITH MAN.
FROM SUCH A SIMPLE-DOUBLE START
UNTIL WE CROWD THE EARTH WITH KIDS,
BUT HAVE ROOM FOR MORE IN HEARTS.
WE DON'T DISPUTE GLORY AND POWER,
BUT WE SOMETIMES CAN WONDER HOW
GOD COULD HANG AN UDDER LIKE HE DID
IF HE HAD HAD TO MILK A COW.

The Adjustment

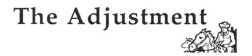

I WALKED REAL SLOW THROUGH THE GRASSES
THAT GLISTENED IN EARLY SUN.
AND I LET THOUGHTS WANDER ALL OVER
ON WHAT NEEDED TO BE DONE.

I WANTED NO INTERFERENCE FOR NOTHING
AND NO ONE WAS TO GET IN MY WAY.
I HAD A WORLD GOING THROUGH MY HEAD
AND I HEARD NOTHING, AS I STARTED THAT DAY.

AN THEN THAT DARK-FACED FELLOW JERKED
MY ATTENTION AROUND WHERE I'D LOOK.
HE YELLED AT ME IN AN ONEROUS TONE
AND CALLED ME EVERY NAME IN THE BOOK.

HE LET ME KNOW MY LIFE GAVE NO REASON
TO IGNORE HIM OR SHUN OTHER FOLK,
AND HIS TONE SUGGESTED THAT LAUGHING
COULD TURN A TOUGH LIFE TO A JOKE.

WITH LONGER LEGS, I'D HAVE KICKED HIM.
MADE HIM WISH HE'D HAVE BEEN STILL.
NO ONE TALKS TO ME LIKE HE DID THAT MORN
WITHOUT ME BEING READY TO KILL.

BUT HE COCKED HIS HEAD KINDA SIDEWAYS
AND THREW A LAST BARB, WOULD YOU KNOW,
AND I WAS LEFT WITH A SMILE ON MY FACE;
MY BAD ATTITUDE FLEW WITH THAT CROW.

That Old Cow

THERE'S A COW THAT STANDS IN MY BEDROOM;
I SWEAR TO YOU, THAT IS CORRECT.
AND BEFORE YOU WORRY ABOUT MESSES,
KNOW THAT IT'S ALL CIRCUMSPECT.

EVEN MY WIFE APPROVES OF HER BEING
AND LIKES THE SERVICE SHE GIVES.
THAT OLD COW IS OKAY IN EVERY WAY,
AND WELCOME AS SURE AS WE LIVE.

WE GIVE THAT OLD COW DAILY ATTENTION
AND SHE PRODUCES THINGS FOR OUR GOOD.
HER PRODUCE WE TRADE FOR WHAT'S WANTED
IN FUN OR CLOTHING OR FOOD.

THAT OLD COW MAKES NO DEMANDS WHATSOEVER.
SHE IS DOCILE AND KIND TO THE KIDS.
THERE WILL BE AN INHERITANCE STRUGGLE
WHEN THAT OLD COW IS PUT UP FOR BIDS.

SHE WAS A WEDDING GIFT FROM OUR BISHOP,
A GREAT GIFT FOR THE YOUNG IN LOVE.
THAT OLD COW IS STILL SERVING WELL NOW
THAT WE ARE BOTH GREY UP ABOVE.

SHE'S BEEN THERE THROUGHOUT THE MARRIAGE,
AND SHE AIN'T LIKELY TO LEAVE,
THAT OLD COW IS JUST A PART OF US NOW
AND IS PERMANENT, I DO BELIEVE.

THAT OLD COW IS A FRIEND OF LONG STANDING
AND SERVES VERY WELL EVERY DAY.
SHE NEVER BAWLS, NEITHER SLOBBERS,
NOR DOES SHE CONSUME ANY HAY.

YOU REALLY NEED A COW IN YOUR BEDROOM,
TO ASSIST IN WHEREVER YOU'RE GOIN'.
FOR THAT OLD COW IS A CERAMIC FIXTURE
THAT SERVES AS A COLLECTOR OF COIN!

---

*A cow's temper isn't changed by
cutting off her horns.*

Funerals

EACH TIME WE BURY SOME ONE
WE GATHER ROUND AND WEEP
AND TELL SOME SOME TALES
OF WHAT ALL HE'D DONE
BEFORE HE FELL ASLEEP.

IT AIN'T EXACTLY LIES WE TELL.
FOR THAT WE'RE FAR TOO WISE.
IT'S JUST EMBELLISHED FACTS
THAT CAN'T BE PROVED OR NOT.
OUR JUDGMENTS EXERCISED!

IF THE STORY IS A GOOD ONE,
WE CLAIM IT TO EPITOMIZE
HOW WE SHOULD EVER LIVE
AND ACCEPT OUR HUMBLE FATE;
AND NOT AGGRANDIZE LIES.

THE PARSON SEZ WE EULOGIZE.
OFTEN, WE EMPHASIZE THE BEST
OF WHAT'S REMEMBERED,
AND FANTASIZE SOME MORE
BEFORE WE PLANT THE PEST.

WE DON'T TELL TOO MUCH TRUTH,
LEST PEOPLE SOON SURMISE
THAT GETTIN' TO BE BETTER
AIN'T PRIMARILY THE THING
TO ACCOMPLISH 'FORE ONE DIES.

Two Learning

MY SON AND I LAUGHED TOGETHER
THE DAY HE DISCOVERED ME WRONG.
HE BECAUSE I'D BEEN CORNERED,
AND I 'CAUSE IT TOOK HIM SO LONG.

NO LONGER DID WE CARE WHAT HAD MATTERED
NOR REMEMBER WHAT CAUSED US THE GRIEF.
IT ONLY WAS GOOD BECAUSE TWO MEN STOOD
AND SHARED EACH OTHERS RELIEF.

HE IS NOT A BOY ANY LONGER,
HE'S A BROTHER NOW, AS MUCH AS A SON.
HIS LAUGHTER'S OKAY AT MY FAULTS TODAY,
'CAUSE HIS KID WILL GET HIM, 'FORE IT'S DONE.

Neighbors

WE HAVE LOTS OF GRANGERS THESE DAYS
AND THEY BUY-IN NOW, 'STEAD OF JUST SQUATTIN'.
THEY SETTLE IN AND BECOME KITH AND KIN,
AND PROVIDE US GOOD THINGS, STORE-BOUGHTEN.
THEY'LL NOT LOOT YOUR HOUSE WHILE YOU'RE OUT,
YOU RARELY FIND A COW THAT'S SHOT DEAD,
YOU CAN LEAVE YOUR HOME AND GO FOR A RIDE,
BUT A REAL SMART MAN LOCKS HIS SHED!

The Old Wagon

SPLINTERED AND CRACKED FROM LABOR AND TIME,
WARPED AND WEATHERED AND GREY,
THE OLD WAGON SITS UNDER THE BIG COTTONWOOD
WITH A STORY IT CANNOT SAY.

RETIRED IT HAS BEEN FOR SEVERAL YEARS,
OUT OF SERVICE AND USE,
ON DISPLAY IN THE NEIGHBOR'S FRONT LAWN
AS QUIET AS ANY RECLUSE.

THE KIDS CLIMB, AND PRETEND FROM THE BOARDS,
FEIGNING AUTOS, SHIPS, AND PLANES.
THEY'RE NOT AWARE OF THE PRECEDING LOADS.
HISTORY EARNS ONLY DISDAIN.

THE TALE TO BE TOLD WILL NEVER BE GRASPED;
NO MAN KNOWS IT CLEAR THROUGH.
THE WAGON OUTLIVED ELEVEN STRONG TEAMS
AND NUMEROUS HARVEST CREWS.

A BENT, AGED COUPLE WINKS EACH TIME THEY PASS,
RECALLING A COURTSHIP RIDE.
HAY WAS PILED DEEP AND BLANKETS WERE WARM,
THEY SNUGGLED DEEP INSIDE.

ANOTHER GROUP THINKS OF THE LONG MOVING DAY
WHEN NEW HOUSE TOOK THEM IN,
AND A WAGON STACKED WITH ALL THEY OWNED
CARRIED THEM AND YOUNGER KIN.

AND THE POOR FOLKS WHO OWNED THE WAGON
    BEFORE
HAVE SORROW TO REHEARSE.
THEY HAD NAUGHT WHEN THEIR DEAR DAUGHTER DIED,
SO WAGON SERVED AS A HEARSE.

MANY ARE THE TALES, AND ENCHANTING THE PLOTS,
INTRIGUING THE CHANGING SCENES,
OF A WAGON THAT SERVED FROM A HALT, TO A JOLT
WHEN DRAGGED BY RUN-AWAY TEAMS.

NOW, IT'S ACTION SUSPENDED, AND FLOWER POT FULL,
CONVEYANCE IS ONLY A WISH.
THE WAGON'S NOW SHELTER FOR PRETTY SMALL BIRDS,
OR VISITOR'S PETS ON A LEASH.

THOUGH WOOD WILL ROT OUT AND METAL WILL RUST,
THE WAGON WILL NEVER DEPART.
FOND MEMORIES ARE ETCHED INTO HEAVEN ITSELF,
TO LIVE IN ETERNAL HEARTS.

Write Right

THERE IS NOT MUCH TO WRITING A POEM;
IT'S JUST PUTTING WORDS IN A LINE.
WORDS ARE REAL PLAIN BY THEIR LONESOME,
BUT TOGETHER THEY ARE REALLY SUBLIME.

ONE CAN TELL OF THINGS OF YOUR LIKING,
OR THINGS THAT YOU LOATHE TO THE CORE.
THINGS THAT GRAB THOUGHTS AND EXCITE YOU,
OR THINGS THAT WILL TOTALLY BORE.

ONE CAN WRITE OF PEOPLE AND PLACES
WHERE YOU'VE BEEN OR WANT NOW TO BE,
OR EXTOL THE VIRTUES OF HOME LIFE
AND THE KIDS ON SOMEBODY'S KNEE.

YOU CAN BE QUITE EXACT IN YOUR METRE,
PUT RHYTHM IN EVERY LINE,
OR YOU CAN CHOOSE WORDS EXACTLY,
AND PUT YOUR ATTENTION TO RHYME.

IF YOUR STANDARDS ARE NOT RELENTING,
AND PERFECTION IS WHAT YOU WANT,
THEN DAYS GO BY AS YOU PONDER
THE EXPRESSION OF EVERY THOUGHT.

BUT IF YOU CAN ACCEPT SOME SMALL LICENSE
GIVEN MARGINAL FOLKS LIKE ME,
YOU FIND THAT YOU ARE A POET
IN MINUTES, JUST TRY IT AND SEE!

Poor Wording

THEY USED TO HANG 'EM IN A TREE
ALONG THE ROAD, JUST OUT OF TOWN,
SO ALL HAD EQUAL CHANCE TO SEE,
BEFORE THEY COME TO CUT 'EM DOWN.
THEY WASN'T THIEVES OF HORSES
OR CHICKENS, OR ANYTHING GOOD.
THEY'D SIMPLY HURT THE REPUTATION
OF THE BEST IN THE NEIGHBORGHOOD.
IT DIDN'T MATTER ABOUT THE TRUTH
OF THE NASTY THINGS THEY'D HINTED.
OR IF THE FACTS WERE UNDERSTOOD
BEHIND WHAT THEY HAD PRINTED.

WE DO IT VERY DIFFERENT NOW.
WE HAVE BIG LAWS FOR SLANDER.
NOTHING'S PRINTED STRAIGHT AWAY
THAT STIRS UP LOCAL DANDER.
IF THE WORDS WE USE ARE IN A RHYME
AN EDITOR WILL NOT TRUST US,
THE JUDGE WILL PUT US IN A JAIL,
AND CALL IT POETIC JUSTICE.

Word Workin's

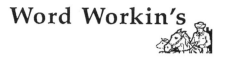

HE LOOKED AT MY PRINTED WORD WORKIN'S
AND HE TRIED TO FEEL WHAT THEY MEANT.
HE WANTED TO MAKE UP SOME POEMS
THAT COULD TO A PRINTER BE SENT.

BUT WHAT HE SAW WAS ONLY MY STYLE
AND ARRANGEMENTS DIDN'T RING TRUE.
HE'D BEEN ON SOME MUCH DIFFERENT OUTFITS,
AND WORKED WITH A MUCH DIFFERENT CREW.

SO HE SAT AND PUT WORDS ON A PAPER
AND STRAIGHTENED AS MUCH AS HE COULD.
HE DIDN'T MIMIC MY PRINTED STUFF
'CAUSE HE WANTED TO DO SOMETHING GOOD!

*When values get to drifting, some
drifter is setting the values.*